C000213550

Some Medieval Records for Family Historians

An Introduction to the
Purposes, Contents and Interpretation
of Pre-1538 Records
Available in Print

PETER FRANKLIN

FEDERATION OF FAMILY HISTORY SOCIETIES

Published by
The Federation of Family History Societies,
The Benson Room, Birmingham, B3 3BS
United Kingdom

First published 1994

ISBN 0-872094-89-9

Printed and bound by Oxuniprint, Walton Street, Oxford OX2 6DP

The Will of Lady Alice West of Hinton Martell, now Dorset, 1395.

In dei nomine, Amen. On thursday, that is to sey, the xv day of the moneth of July, In the yer of the incarnacioun of our lord ihesu crist, a thousand and thre hundred and foure score and fiftene, I, Alice West, lady of Hynton Martel, in hool estat of my body and in good mynde beynge, make my testament in the maner as hit folweth here after,

In the begynnyng, I bequethe my soule to god almyghty and to his moder seynt Marie, and to al the seyntis of hevene, and my body to be beryed in Crischerch in the Priorie of the Chanones in Hamptschire, by the Newe forest, whereas myne Auncestres liggeth,

Also I devyse to Thomas my sone, a bed of tapicers werk, with alle the tapites of sute, red of colour, ypouthered with chapes and scochons, in the corners, of myn Auncestres armes, with that, I bequethe to the same Thomas, the stoffe longyng therto, that is to seye, my best fetherbed, and a blu canevas, and a materas, and twey blankettys, and a peyre schetes of Reynes, with the heved shete of the same, and sex of my best pilwes...

A fine example of a medieval will in English. Note that the first bequest is of the lady's soul, and how quickly the references to her noble ancestors follow upon it!

To Mark and David

Contents

Introduction

The first English parish registers began to be kept in the year 1538 by order of Henry VIII's minister, Thomas Cromwell. Their appearance was such an important development in the keeping of records that if we wanted to take one particular year as marking the end of the Middle Ages and the start of modern times then, from the family historians' viewpoint, a much stronger case could be made for 1538 than for the 1485 beloved of old textbooks, or (perhaps) for any other date.

It is said that the average family historian never looks at any record which pre-dates that watershed. The reasons for this are probably complicated. It is certainly a challenge to trace a family all the way back to Henry VIII's reign *and then further.* Yet there are a whole variety of informative medieval sources which the keen family historian could use, if only he (or she) were aware of their possibilities.

I suspect that there are three main reasons why these sources so often lie unused, namely (1) the belief that surviving medieval documents are rare, (2) a related belief that such documents are only concerned with the famous and the powerful, and (3) the belief that even if records survive which would be useful to the family historian, it will be impossible to make sense of them because their meanings will be hidden behind strange handwriting, the Latin language, and the obscure purposes of the men (probably monks) who wrote them.

This little book aims to show that *all* these beliefs are false. Medieval records survive in great quantities. They are concerned with people from all parts of society. It is true that reading the original manuscripts calls for technical expertise, but many records have been made available in printed versions through the good work of record societies and individuals. It is also true that many were written in Latin (though the local clerk wrote far more than the monks ever did) and some in 'Anglo-French', but many are available in English translations or can be usefully consulted after only a brief acquaintance with the original language. In the later part of the Middle Ages some records were actually written in English, and these will usually pose few problems to modern readers.

This booklet aims to provide the family historian with a practical introduction to the use of several of the kinds of medieval record which are likely to be of most use to him (or her). It is aimed principally at the reader who wants to look at some of the many medieval records which are now in print *in translation,* so it does not offer a guide to palaeography, a Latin grammar or an Anglo-French glossary. (People who wish to learn to read original medieval records may like to begin by looking at L.C. Hector, *The Handwriting of English Documents,* (2nd edn., 1966) and D. Stuart, *Manorial Records. An introduction to their transcription and translation,* (1992). H.E.P. Grieve, *Examples of English Handwriting, 1150-1750,* (1954) is also very useful.)

What this booklet does offer is an introduction to records made for the government, for lords of manors, for the Church and for ordinary people, concentrating on the purposes, contents and interpretation of each. I have devoted one chapter to each kind of record (or to records which are closely related) and have provided for it a brief introduction, to set it in its historical context, followed by accounts of the purpose for which it was made, how it was made, the kinds of people who appear in it, the geographical coverage which it provides and the dates when it was produced, how often it has survived, and the pitfalls of which readers should be aware when working with it.

I have also added for each chapter a Short Bibliography which lists good examples of published records of that kind, both in the original language and in English translation, and which also gives titles of selected studies which describe and discuss that kind of record, or which have put it to some particular use.

Chapter 1

Medieval Records and Medieval Society

The Scope and Availability of Medieval Records

Record-making was one of the great industries of Medieval England which has never received its proper due. Thousands of clerks worked to produce a wide variety of documents for the government, for the Church, for lords of manors and for ordinary townsmen and peasants. As the generations passed, so their numbers grew larger and their pens grew ever busier with lists of lords and tenants, reports of the findings of inquiries, accounts of tenants' lands and obligations, notes of the results of court cases, grants of land, lists of taxpayers' names, wills, and a host of other documents.

Many of these records have been lost over the centuries, yet enormous numbers still survive — so many that no one has ever tried to count them. We will always wish that there were even more, but we are very lucky in comparison with other parts of Europe where war and revolution have destroyed infinitely more. The records which do survive provide a matchless store of information for historians of all kinds, pursuing all kinds of interests. Family historians have probably made less use of them than any other group, but it is to be hoped that this situation will begin to change as growing numbers realise the range of material which is available.

All kinds of people appear in medieval records: kings, nobles, clergymen of all ranks from the greatest archbishops down to the humblest parish priests and chaplains, rich merchants and poor craftsmen, the country gentry, and the peasants — both freemen and serfs — from the prosperous 'franklins' down to poor cottagers. In the documents made for ordinary individuals we shall meet these people only in small numbers, in manorial records we may meet hundreds of them, while in some kinds of government record their names are listed literally by the thousand.

Much of this information has been made far more accessible by the publication of medieval records of particular interest. The appearance of a printed text of *Domesday Book* in the late eighteenth century was a milestone in this process. Since then, many national records have been printed by H.M.S.O. and many local ones by county record societies and, sometimes, by private or commercial publishers. This work goes on today at a faster pace than ever.

These publications have put a tremendous wealth of information at the family historian's fingertips. The practical difficulties involved in having to read original documents in medieval hands, and in the Latin or Anglo-French of clerks who often used archaic systems of abbreviating words, have been eliminated. So — on a very practical note — have much of the trouble and expense of long journeys to record offices and specialist libraries, for most of these publications can be consulted in ordinary reference libraries or borrowed through the Inter-Library Loans service.

Large numbers of useful documents are readily available. One barrier is down, but another remains: now that the family historian has ready access to these sources, what is he (or she) to do with them? The records survive in bewildering varieties. Some may have been encountered before because they continued to be produced into the modern period, but it will be unclear whether they *meant* the same in the Middle Ages. Many others will be quite unfamiliar. Some will be the products of institutions, administrative practices and habits of thought which have long since disappeared.

It is the aim of this little book to provide a guide to their contents, purposes and interpretation.

A Brief Introduction to Medieval Society

Medieval records grew out of medieval conditions and ideas, in order to answer medieval purposes. Though some kinds continued to be drawn up until well into the modern period, they were designed to fulfill the needs of members of a completely different kind of society, a vanished world where whole government departments had once travelled round the country on the backs of pack-horses, and where it had made sense to despatch small armies of amateur taxmen to collect silver pennies from the peasant inhabitants of scattered hamlets and farmsteads.

So many of our old records are about landed property and country people because Medieval England was rural to a degree which is now hard to believe. A population which probably never exceeded six or seven millions lived mostly in rural settlements, and very often in hamlets and isolated farmsteads rather than in anything large enough to be called a 'village'. London was the only place big enough to rank alongside the great continental cities, and its population may not have exceeded 40,000 or 50,000. Provincial 'capitals' like Bristol and York had about 10,000 inhabitants, and many country towns no more than a few hundred, although the markets, fairs and administrative functions of the towns gave them great importance.

We can divide the people of medieval England up into three social classes, namely, the ruling class, the townsmen and the peasantry.

The Ruling Class

The ruling class was principally made up of the warrior elite, the king, nobles and gentry who liked to see themselves as the heirs of William the Conqueror and his knights. We can see them from different points of view. From the military point of view, they were the mounted knights; from the economic point of view the lords of manors; from the political point of view the rulers of the country. In the last resort their power rested upon the skill in warfare to which they were trained from childhood, though (as the centuries passed) increasing numbers of them took no part in warfare but functioned as private holders of estates or served as county administrators, judges, and so on, for the king. Members of the medieval ruling class varied tremendously in their importance: a small group were the great barons, sometimes having close blood ties with the royal family. Most were of far less importance, and historians have taken to extending the term 'country gentry' back in time to cover these lords of a few manors who were important people only in their own local districts and who might not have bothered to get themselves knighted. For most of our period they also retained a major cultural role as the patrons of artists and craftsmen of all kinds.

This elite was held together by the network of 'feudal' relationships established by the Conqueror and his successors. Each lord was not the 'owner' of his estates, but was said to 'hold' his lands from his superior lord by performing obligations to the latter. (The Middle Ages did not like to think of land as something which could be *owned,* in the same way that a man could own an ox or a bushel of wheat, though references to it being 'bought' and 'sold' do occur in documents.) Often these were obligations of a military nature, such as helping to guard the superior lord's castle or fighting for him on horseback. In return, the overlord provided his inferior, or 'vassal', with the support and protection much needed in a violent world. The king himself stood at the top of the feudal tree. All land was ultimately held of him, the overlord of all overlords who could call upon the allegiance of all lords of manors.

In William I's day this arrangement provided the king with an up-to-date army of several thousand mounted knights. As the centuries passed its military provisions were much diluted as the changing requirements of warfare made it better to hire professional soldiers than to call the country gentry to the colours, but the basic arrangement remained in place throughout our period and continued to affect the making and keeping of records.

The Townsmen

The merchants and craftsmen of the towns were people of much less consequence. Yet each town had its little elite of successful men, often linked by family ties and by membership of church guilds which had ostensibly religious ends. Local elites ran the towns, with occasional challenges from groups of ordinary craftsmen, the 'small masters' with their own workshops. The divisions within the townsmen were every bit as great as those within the other classes. Every urban community had large numbers of poor, and as time passed the wage workers were becoming a more important part of the population.

Medieval towns and cities were tiny, yet their functions as centres of trade and production (making everything which the country craftsman could not produce) were vital. Each town had a privileged position: though the inhabitants might still pay their rent to the great lord who had granted their settlement borough status (and whom they would be wise not to offend) townsmen did have their own rights or 'liberties', to use a word which the Middle Ages loved. Running most of their own affairs, they served as market centres for the surrounding rural areas, and held fairs which might draw people from many miles away (in some cases even from overseas). Large numbers of towns were given independent status, especially in the thirteenth century, by lords who were fully prepared to grant their inhabitants a large share of self-rule and to acknowledge their special status in return for a swollen rent roll and toll payments from the trade done in the marketplace. Although most medieval towns were small in size, they formed a network of trading, production and administrative centres which covered the whole country.

The Peasants

But the medieval English were overwhelmingly a peasant nation. Ninety per cent or more of them were peasants living on their family holdings of land and getting much or all of their incomes by cultivating these to produce their own food, in the form of corn, vegetables, fruit and animal products. This pattern of peasant economy with a large element of 'self-sufficiency' was a very old one, and it was slowly breaking down during the Middle Ages as differences of wealth and kind of family economy spread through the peasantry. All peasants were by no means equal at the time of the Norman Conquest. There were already great differences in the amounts of land which peasant families held. At the top of the tree, rich peasants had so much land that they could produce a regular surplus of corn and other produce to take to market and sell. Those with only a little land scraped a living by working for the better off, who could not cultivate their large holdings with only the labour of their own families. Poor peasants like these had to buy the food which they did not have enough land to grow. Between the two groups there were still plenty of middle peasants, living a life of basic self-sufficiency and able to grow enough food on their pieces of land to feed their families. Other differences were also appearing within the peasantry, as increasing numbers of people began to make much of their livings by practising crafts and trades rather than just by producing food.

Freedom and Serfdom

The peasants had fallen under the power of their local lords, who were their landlords and to whom they owed a wide range of obligations and payments. To a large degree, this had happened before the Norman Conquest ever took place. But the power of the lords strengthened and the position of many peasants weakened about a century after the Conquest when many peasants fell into serfdom, or 'villeinage' as it was often called in England.

Serfs suffered very real disabilities, but the popular notion that serfdom itself condemned people to great poverty is false. Indeed, it was to the lord of the manor's advantage to have reasonably well-off peasants as his serfs, those who could afford to take time off from working their own land in order to work his, and who could bring their own plough-oxen with them. Nor were serfs cut off from the record-making process: like other peasants they could make their wills and give and receive land by charter, whatever some older textbooks might say on the subject. Nor did being a serf get you off from paying taxes to the king's Exchequer.

The Place of the Church

The clergy occupied a very special place within this class structure. Each of the three classes contained a clerical element. The great archbishops, bishops and abbots were clearly members of the ruling class, while the local priests and chaplains in the towns and in the countryside are best considered as members of the townsmen and of the peasantry.

In medieval society, the processes of record-making and record-preserving were largely the work of the clergy, especially in the first centuries after the Conquest. 'Clerk' and 'cleric' are really the same word, and date from a time when it was assumed that a literate person would be in holy orders, though not necessarily that he would be a priest. One of the great worldly functions of the medieval church was to supply lay society with educated, literate administrators. For centuries, it was common practice for some of the bishops to double as royal ministers. The angry insurgents of 1381 did not execute the Archbishop of Canterbury because he was a great churchman, but because he was the Chancellor of the Exchequer. The first English government to exclude senior churchmen was an ignominious failure, incapable of properly implementing the new tax it had planned. Clergymen continued to act as advisors to the nobility on a whole range of practical subjects, and working as a chaplain and secretary in a gentry family was a good job for a minor cleric. Fifteenth-century gentry like Sir John Fastolf and the Paston family had chaplains who filled this double role.

The church was also heavily involved in preserving both its own records and other people's. Indeed, it had a head start over any family of laymen in that it could not die and was most unlikely to have its property stolen or confiscated. As a corporation which carried on from one generation to the next, with, usually, fairly smooth transitions of power from one office-holder to the next, it was well-placed to preserve records of all kinds. Many of the surviving medieval records which we would not think of as being at all 'ecclesiastical' have survived because they were in the hands of the church. Churchmen kept local records relating to the manors belonging to their bishoprics or abbeys — such as the surveys and court records described in later chapters — which were just like the same records kept by noblemen and gentry and relating to their manors. What is the difference? The great practical difference is that the churchmen's records are much more likely to have survived, because they were carefully preserved, away from the damp and the rats, and — perhaps more importantly — away from the numerous accidents and dangers of family life and unsuccessful rebellion in turbulent times.

True, at the end of the Middle Ages the English abbeys lost their manors, as, indeed, did many smaller religious institutions, while many bishoprics also lost much of their property. But by that time a new breed of nobleman and gentleman had grown up, one who was anxious not just to get his hands onto more manors, but to secure and preserve all the written documents which went with them, all the scraps of old parchment and paper which might secure his rights to new property all the more firmly, and which might prove his title to valuable local rights of all kinds. C. Rawcliffe (1976) shows us an example of such a man.

A Tri-lingual Country

The Anglo-Saxons had used their own language, 'Old English', for a wide variety of administrative and literary purposes. It was the Norman Conquest which made England into a country of three main languages, where the ruling class spoke and wrote Anglo-Norman (or Anglo-French), churchmen used Medieval Latin, royal officers and administrators used both those languages, and the illiterate mass of the population clung to English.

King Harold's defeat robbed his people's language of its status until the days of Geoffrey Chaucer. It ushered in the curious world (very strange to the monoglot English of today) where people from different origins used different languages according to what purpose they were about. Clerks of French birth toured England to compile Domesday Book in Latin, and must have had great fun trying to write down English place-names and personal names. Many kinds of government record went into Latin and stayed there, though in many cases this did not mean that the clerks had to have a very great mastery of the language. It is an open secret that many kinds of medieval Latin record make much use of standard phrases, while the lists of taxpayers' names drawn up for the Exchequer are 'in Latin' only to the extent that the clerks have Latinized people's names, turning 'Robert Carpenter' into *Robertus Carpentarius.*

Court records suffered an odd fate. The major royal courts began to keep records of their proceedings in Anglo-French and continued to do this after that language declined at the end of the Middle Ages. Anglo-French eventually turned into 'Law French', and continued as an extraordinary survival, learned and used only by lawyers practising in the courts at Westminster. Manorial courts, however, kept their records in Latin and continued to do so beyond the end of our period – in fact, as late as the year 1733.

The different kinds of private documents made for ordinary people might be made in any of these languages. Most were made in Latin, until the revival of English was reflected in the making of large numbers of English wills in the last part of the period.

The Dating of Records

This little book is aimed principally at users of published records, and the editors of published volumes have generally given the dates of the documents which they have printed in modern form. But some publications (especially older ones) leave dates in their original forms.

It is by no means unusual for some kinds of medieval record to be dated by day, month and year A.D.. The system of reckoning years from the birth of Christ is itself a medieval invention. The Venerable Bede was one of the first historians to date events by the Year of Grace – the 'Year of Our Lord' or 'A.D.', which simply stands for the Latin *Anno Domini.*

Many other medieval records are dated by regnal years. Many readers will have met this system before, as it was widely used for official documents in later times. (It is still used to date Acts of Parliament.) Regnal years do not correspond to years A.D.. The oldest practice was for the start of the king's reign to be taken as the date of his coronation. This was logical because it was at that ceremony that he made his formal promise to govern his people well and was accepted by them as king, but it broke down in 1272 when Henry III died and his successor was 2,000 miles away on crusade. It was two years before Edward I returned and his coronation took place. After that date, the first day of each new reign was generally taken to be either the last day of the previous one, or the day next after that.

Documents made for a bishop, including manorial records from his estates, may employ a curious variant of this. They may be dated by the year of the bishop's 'pontificate' (which sounds very grand, but is the right word). But they will usually also show the regnal year or the year A.D.

Documents and events may be dated by reference to saints' days, e.g. to 'the eve of St Martin in Winter' or to 'Monday next after the feast of St Lucy the Virgin'. Feast days can be divided into two kinds: the fixed ones which fall upon the same day and month every year, and those which are movable. Fixed feasts are easy with the help of a textbook. St Martin in Winter (or 'Martinmas') is always 11 November, and St Lucy the Virgin is always the 13 December. It is the movable feasts, of which the greatest is Easter, which pose the problems. Easter Day (or 'Easter Sunday') can fall on any date between the 22 March and the 25 April.

Dating by reference to saints' days and regnal years looks complicated at first, but a number of handbooks are available. I would recommend C.R. Cheney (1970) which contains tables of regnal years, lists of saints' days, and ingenious calendars for every year from A.D.500 to A.D.2000.

Where should we begin?

Where should a little book of this kind begin? The Anglo-Saxons liked family history of a rather specialised kind. One version of their great *Chronicle* begins by tracing the line of the West Saxon kings back from King Alfred and his successors to the god Woden. But the prospects of using this source seem to be thin for most of us.

The records which are most likely to be of use to the family historian do not begin until after the Norman Conquest. Many of the lords of manors' and private records do not survive in substantial numbers until the thirteenth or fourteenth centuries, so that for the first part of the period we have to rely largely upon government records.

For that reason I have chosen to take Domesday Book as my starting point. It offers coverage of almost the whole of England. Many families have claimed descent from the people who 'came over with the Conqueror', and we should expect to find many of their names in its pages. Also, there are so many misconceptions about what is actually in the great Book that it seems best to start by clearing them up.

SHORT BIBLIOGRAPHY

I have listed useful books on the social history of the period, rather than those which concentrate on political events. (The latter are covered at length in the volumes of the Oxford History of England.)

Keen (1990), Myers (1971) and Stenton (1965) provide excellent introductions to medieval society.

Books on Medieval Records and Medieval Society

C.R. Cheney, ed., *Handbook of Dates for Students of English History,* Royal Hist. Soc. Guides and Handbooks No.4 (1970).

M.T. Clanchy, *From Memory to Written Record. England 1066-1307,* (2nd edn., 1993).

F. & J. Gies, *Life in a Medieval Village,* (1990).

C. Given-Wilson, *The English Nobility in the Late Middle Ages: The Fourteenth-Century Political Community,* (1987).

R. Hilton, *The Decline of Serfdom in Medieval England,* (1970).

G.C. Homans, *English Villagers of the Thirteenth Century,* (Cambridge, Mass., 1941).

M. Keen, *English Society in the Later Middle Ages, 1348-1500,* (1990).

A.R. Myers, *England in the Late Middle Ages,* (8th edn., 1971).

M.M. Postan, *The Medieval Economy and Society. An Economic History of Britain in the Middle Ages,* (1972).

E. Power, *Medieval People,* (10th edn., 1963).

E. Power, *Medieval Women,* (ed. M.M. Postan, 1975).

C. Rawcliffe, 'A Tudor Nobleman as Archivist: The Papers of Edward, Third Duke of Buckingham', *Journal of Soc. of Archivists,* v (1976), pp. 294-300.

D.M. Stenton, *English Society in the Early Middle Ages (1066-1307),* (4th edn., 1965).

Chapter 2

Domesday Book, with a Note on the Manor

Introduction: The Norman Survey of England

Medieval England was a profoundly rural country. The great majority of its people (probably more than 90 per cent of them) were peasants living on their family holdings, getting their livings by working their arable land and tending their livestock, and owing rent and other obligations to the local lord of the manor. The Norman Conquest replaced the Anglo-Saxon lords by foreigners, and introduced the developed continental system of feudal relationships between greater and lesser lords, drawing everyone into a chain of landholding which stretched all the way from the king at its summit down to the peasants at its base.

Besides a new aristocracy, the Normans brought with them the custom of making written records in Latin and a remarkable administrative capacity. The last is best remembered today because of its greatest achievement, the Domesday Book which offers a survey of almost the whole of the kingdom which William I had conquered, in a form so systematic that it could be contained within two volumes.

The Purpose of the Record

The Book is a huge and complex record. It does not declare what its exact purpose was and there has been plenty of scholarly debate about this. The great pioneering medieval historians F.W. Maitland and J.H. Round believed that it was essentially a 'geld book', or source for making tax assessments. Certainly it says much about the resources of the Conqueror's subjects, and new taxation may have been one thing in his mind, but it also forms a comprehensive guide to the new feudal structure of England and a repository of evidence about how much land the mass of ordinary Englishmen held and the conditions on which they held it. We should perhaps interpret the words of the Anglo-Saxon Chronicle (a record which continued to be written for two generations after the Conquest) that the king wanted to know, 'about this land, how it was peopled, and with what sort of men', as a request for a wide-ranging social and economic survey, for that is one of the things which Domesday Book is.

The Domesday Survey was basically an enquiry into the landholding and economic resources of the king's subjects and into their places in the feudal hierarchy. It was not restricted to how matters stood in 1086, but also concerned itself with the situation which had existed before the Conqueror's momentous reign and with the changes which had taken place during it.

The enormous amount of information in Domesday Book, the certified accuracy of that information, and its handy arrangement by counties and lords' estates made it of great use as a reference book for disputes over feudal rights and obligations. Its record quickly acquired great authority not only amongst lawyers, but amongst the native English who saw its verdict as being as fixed and authoritative as that of the scriptural Judgement Day — the great day of Doom, hence the popular name which made its first appearance in official records in 1221. Indeed, E.M. Hallam (1986) argues that its reputation became over-inflated and quotes cases of its testimony being cited in matters on which it had nothing to say.

The Making of the Record

The story of how the survey came to be undertaken is told in the Anglo-Saxon Chronicle. William I spent Christmas 1085 at Gloucester, and had discussions with his counsellors about the make-up of England, after which he sent out his Commissioners to gather information about the country.

The officers who made the survey, who have generally become known as 'Commissioners', worked by counties and by the manors within each county — except in remote areas where this was not feasible. Beginning with the king's own manors, they carefully noted the name of each lord of the manor, how many tenants he had, how much agricultural land both lord and peasants had, what livestock they owned, what corn mills, woods, and so on, there were within each manor. The wide-ranging scope and thoroughness of the enquiry led to complaints noted in the Anglo-Saxon Chronicle.

Some historians believe that it is possible to trace distinct 'circuits' which groups of Domesday Commissioners followed and so to divide up the country into several regions, each of which was surveyed by a different 'team'. The information was then brought to a central office, reduced to a standard, abbreviated form and then compiled to make the planned Book.

But this plan was never finished: the king died in September 1087, and the Book shows signs of having been completed in a hurry. The information from the three eastern counties of Norfolk, Suffolk and Essex was not condensed in the usual way, but was bound together to form a second volume, while that from all the other counties was fitted into volume one. This is the origin of the division of the survey's text into 'Great Domesday', which covers 37 counties, and 'Little Domesday' which covers only three, but in much greater detail.

A Note on the Manor

As you read through the text of Domesday Book, you will quickly become aware that its makers had an interest in 'manors' which varied from the keen to the obsessive. They divide as much of the country as they can into manors, and then procede to tell us about each one — what its name is, who its lord was in 1066, who its lord is now, how many corn mills he has and how much land, how many tenants he has, what kind of people they are and how much land they hold.

The manor was one of the basic building blocks of medieval society. As such, it played a major role in the lives of many people and manorial institutions (especially the manor court) became major producers of records.

A manor was, quite simply, an estate belonging to a member of the ruling class. The lord of the manor held it of his superior lord (who might be the king himself), very often 'by knight service', the obligation to go and fight for his superior lord in time of war. Its boundaries might be the same as those of the local parish, but this was by no means always so. The manor might include only part of the parish, or part of this parish and part of the next one. Nor need the land of the manor always stand together in one solid block. A small manor might be made up of little 'islands' of property spread out across the 'sea' of another, larger, manor.

Manors varied tremendously in size, from (say) a hundred acres up to many thousands of acres. Text books have always concentrated on large ones, partly because their records have been more likely to survive. The sizes of manors tended to reflect the status of their lords, for there was a tendency for the greatest nobles to have very large manors covering many square miles, and for ordinary 'gentry' to have only medium or small ones covering a few hundred acres. The numbers of manors a lord might have varied tremendously: a small gentleman might have only one, a great earl might have dozens, spread across several counties. Besides acting as feudal overlord of everyone else's manors, the king had literally hundreds of manors of his own.

The manor provided its lord with his status and income, and in order to achieve the latter it was divided into two portions. Domesday Book provides only thumb-nail sketches of each manor, but the *Manorial Surveys* of later centuries give more details of this division into 'demesne' and tenants' land. The lord has his manor house (it may be a castle, or a collection of domestic buildings standing cheek-by-jowl with the barns and byres), and he has a garden, an orchard, a corn mill, a fishpond, a warren (where rabbits and game birds are bred for hunting), a dovecot (which also provides fresh meat), and a bit of private woodland, which in the centuries after 1086 he may well have converted into a deer park. Here are all the things needed for a gentleman's life in the country. In order to provide him and his family with food and money income, a part of the agricultural land of the manor is set aside for his use and not let out to tenants. The crops grown on this land may be eaten by the lord and his family or sold at the nearest market. These amenities and lands, the parts of the manor which the lord keeps to use himself, are called his 'demesne'.

The rest of the land of the manor — arable land, meadow, pasture and woodland — is let out to tenants, most or all of whom are local peasants. They pay the lord money rent for these lands which (from their point of view) make up their family holdings, and they often have the obligation to go along and work the lord's demesne for him. This is how much of the work of growing the lord's own crops and tending his animals is done, by the unpaid labour which his tenants do for him *as well as* paying him rent in modern fashion. The lord also has a 'demesne staff' of men and women who live at his manor house, or close by, and who work for him full time. These are the slaves who appear in Domesday Book. In later times they are serfs chosen from the local peasant community.

As lord of the manor, a member of the ruling class is in a far stronger position than any mere squire or landlord of later centuries. He is the local representative of the ruling, warrior class, and he has rights and powers which later landlords might well envy. He can compel local people to do unpaid work for him and

The land of William, son of Ansculf.

In Saisdon Hundred:

William, son of Ansculf, holds Segleslei of the king. Earl Algar held it. There are six hides there, land for twelve ploughs. There is one ploughland in demesne and three slaves, with 45 villeins and a priest and two bordars who have 18 ploughs. There are 16 acres of meadow. There is woodland two leagues long and one wide. It was worth £10 in King Edward's time; it is now worth the same.

The same William holds three hides in Penne, and Gilbert holds of him. Countess Godiva held them. There is land for six ploughs. There is one ploughland in demesne, and six villeins with one freeman have one and a half ploughlands. There are four acres of meadow there. It is worth 20s.

The same William holds another five hides in Penne, and Robert holds of him. Earl Algar held them. There is land for six ploughs. There is one ploughland in demesne with one slave, and eight villeins and two bordars with one ploughland. There is a mill there at 2s. It was and is worth 30s.

The same William holds three hides in Overtone, and Walbert holds of him. Wulfstan held them, and he was a free man. There is land for four ploughs. There are two ploughlands in demesne with two slaves, and seven villeins and two bordars with two ploughlands. There are four acres of meadow there. It was and is worth 40s.

Figure 1. Brief descriptions from Domesday Book of some of the manors of a Staffordshire nobleman, naming his vassals and the pre-Conquest lords and ladies. 'Countess Godiva' is the famous Lady Godiva.

make them bring their corn to his mill to be ground, so that he takes the profit. He can extract a bewildering range of payments from local people who, as the generations pass, run the risk of falling into serfdom and themselves becoming his property. As time passes, he may be able to help himself to some of the local community's resources, such as by converting woodland into a private deer park. He can even hold his own private court of law, the manor court, where he himself (or his chosen representative) can sit in judgement on local people and add their fines to his personal income! Indeed, the right to hold a manor court gradually came to be seen as a test of whether someone possessed a true manor, with all its rights, or just a collection of properties.

Readers should be warned that in some parts of the country manorial terminology breaks down. This is especially true in the North of England where some really huge manors existed. These were often known as 'baronies' or 'honors' (a word which in usual medieval parlance meant a collection of manors). The De Lacy family's great 'Honor of Clitheroe' was one huge manor covering about one-sixth of Lancashire. Local records sometimes divided it into several parts, which could themselves be referred to as 'manors', but the divisions were not permanent and it makes most sense to consider the whole edifice as one gigantic manor. And, indeed, it was no larger than the great Manor of Wakefield, just over the Yorkshire border.

Kinds of People Appearing

No fewer than 275,000 people appear in Domesday Book, but the bad news is that most of them are not named. Those who are named are the members of the ruling class, the nobles, bishops and abbots, and the many ordinary lords of manors who were holding estates in 1086, along with their predecessors who occupied the same positions in 1066. The tenants who held land on each manor, the mass of the population, remain anonymous: the Book only recorded that there were so many people of each particular kind, so many 'villeins', 'cottars', 'bordars', and so on.

(Note that the word 'villeins' changed its meaning during the Middle Ages. In 1086 it meant 'substantial peasants', but after the growth of serfdom it became widely used as a synonym for 'serfs'. 'Cottars' and 'bordars' were peasants with little land.)

Geographical Coverage and Dates

No fewer than 13,418 places are named in the great Book. Although we count Domesday as a great *national* record, it does not cover the whole of England. The four northernmost counties — Cumberland, Westmorland, Northumberland and Durham — were not surveyed, except for a few settlements mentioned below. In 1086 these counties did not yet exist, nor was it clear that this northern region would become a fixed part of the English kingdom. The northern border was only established in the time of William Rufus (who founded Carlisle Castle) and Henry II. It is unlikely that this region was excluded because it had suffered attacks from both the Conqueror's men and from the Scots, because other devastated parts of the North of England were surveyed.

(Much of County Durham and some parts of Northumberland were surveyed for the Bishop of Durham in 1183. The result, called 'Boldon Book', is reminiscent of Domesday Book, and has been included both in the edition of Domesday completed by the Record Commissioners and as a volume of Phillimore's modern edition. But it only surveys estates held by the Bishop himself whereas Domesday set out to describe everyone's lands.)

Readers must also bear in mind that the 'historic' county boundaries which existed prior to 1974 were not set in stone. Changes took place over the centuries, and you may have to look at the entries for adjacent counties to find the person or place you seek. Lancastrians may be scandalised to find that their county did not yet exist in 1086. Part of it appears in a special section headed 'Between the Ribble and the Mersey' (printed in Phillimore's Cheshire volume), and the rest is included with Yorkshire. The Domesday account of Yorkshire also includes a few places which were later parts of Cumberland and Westmorland. Nor did the Welsh border stand just where it stood in later times, and much of what would become the county of Flint is counted in with Cheshire. If you are looking for a named person or place and are unsure of the county, then Phillimore's new indexes of personal names and place-names will be of great assistance.

Coverage of cities is one of the Survey's weak points. The Commissioners were much more at home in the world of manors than in the urban settlements of King William's England. What they have to say about such places is interesting, but the largest cities seem to have caused them great problems, and London and Bristol are among those which simply do not appear in their record.

The Commissioners began their work some time after Christmas 1085. William I died on 9 September 1087, and there are signs that the final stages of the great project were completed in a hurry.

We should always bear in mind that they enquired not only about how things stood in the mid-1080s, but also about conditions at the very end of Edward the Confessor's reign, which was 5 January 1066 ('the day when King Edward was alive and dead').

Survival

Domesday Book is unique among the records discussed in this booklet because only one copy was made, because it has enjoyed a 100 per cent 'survival rate', and because its custodians will not allow us to consult the original document *under any circumstances whatsoever.*

Its first home was in Winchester; in the reign of King John (1199-1216) it was moved to the Exchequer at Westminster. The medieval government often moved about, taking its money and records with it in carts and on pack-horses. We know that Domesday Book sometimes went with it, and we may be thankful that it survived the risks of loss and serious damage. It was transferred to the newly-opened Public Record Office in Chancery Lane in 1859, and has since been allowed few excursions. It went to Southampton to be photographed in the early 1860s, and was a wartime evacuee, spending World War One at Bodmin and World War Two at Shepton Mallet.

The Book is displayed in the P.R.O. Museum, where we may look but we may not touch. And, indeed, for the past 200 years we have had no need to, for Abraham Farley produced a magnificent printed edition of its text in two volumes during the reign of George III. (This edition is often associated with the name of the Record Commissioners. They were not set up until nearly twenty years later, but their name appeared on the copies of Farley's edition which remained, and two further volumes of indexes and of other records associated with Domesday were produced under their auspices − hence the confusion.) Farley's edition (which contains no translation of the abbreviated and technical Latin text) can still be found in very large libraries. But in recent years it has become practical for ordinary public libraries and individual family and local historians to obtain copies of its text for the counties which interest them *complete with an English translation,* for Phillimore has produced a full set of county volumes with Farley's printed text on the left-hand pages and a modern English translation on the right-hand ones. Each of these county volumes has useful indexes. On a practical note, the new volumes are of a handy size, whereas the Georgian ones look and feel as though they were intended to be used by trainee weightlifters. (Not that users of the St Catherine's House indexes will have any problems with them.)

The original Book has been rebound a number of times over the years, most recently in 1984-86 when the two volumes which had been handed down through the ages were taken apart and reassembled as five. H. Forde (1986) describes the processes and offers a fascinating account of the care and treatment of 900-year-old parchment books.

Pitfalls

Domesday Book's reputation has grown over the centuries, as E.M. Hallam's study shows, and this has sometimes had odd consequences. Some people expect it to be a repository of all known wisdom, whereas in fact it is a 2,000,000-word long survey of eleventh-century England — no more, and no less. It will not mention your house, nor the old oak tree on your village green (even if they are old enough), but it does contain a mass of information about people and places. It certainly has its technicalities, but it was meant to be understood, and modern translations and guides are readily available.

It is important to begin a guide of this kind with this great national record, but it must always be born in mind that it is separated by generations — and in some cases by centuries — from the other kinds of document which can be of service to the family historian. This, of course, will make it more difficult to make satisfactory links between individuals, but consulting the great Book will enable you to do a number of things. If your family has a tradition of an ancestor mentioned in Domesday — if it is one of the many which has claimed descent from one of those who 'came over with the Conqueror', or one of the smaller number acknowledging an ancestor deprived of his estates by the invaders — you will at least be able to look for people of the right name, and what is recorded for them should help you to assess the likely truth of the story more clearly. If your family is believed to come from a particular part of the country at an early period, then the record of Domesday will probably give you the earliest insights into what conditions were like in that area. In this case, the books edited by H.C. Darby and his co-workers (1954-67) will be found to be very useful.

Be careful if you are looking up a common name.

On a minor point, please do ensure that you use the traditional spelling, odd though it is. 'Doomsday' is the meaning, but *Domesday* has long had the full weight of custom behind it.

SHORT BIBLIOGRAPHY

The complete text of Domesday Book was edited by A. Farley in the 1780s, and volumes of indexes and additional material were later published by the Record Commissioners. Major libraries often have copies, but the printed text of that edition is reproduced much more conveniently (and with a full English translation) in the recent 38-volume edition edited by John Morris and published by Phillimore.

Published Domesday Book in Latin and English translation

J. Morris, gen.ed., *Domesday Book,* (Phillimore, Chichester, 1975-92, 38 vols.).

N.B. The volume nos., which follow the order of the Book's text, are as follows;-

1.	Kent	2.	Sussex
3.	Surrey	4.	Hampshire
5.	Berkshire	6.	Wiltshire
7.	Dorset	8.	Somerset
9.	Devon (in two parts)	10.	Cornwall
11.	Middlesex	12.	Hertfordshire
13.	Buckinghamshire	14.	Oxfordshire
15.	Gloucestershire	16.	Worcestershire
17.	Herefordshire	18.	Cambridgeshire
19.	Huntingdonshire	20.	Bedfordshire
21.	Northamptonshire	22.	Leicestershire
23.	Warwickshire	24.	Staffordshire

25. Shropshire	26. Cheshire
27. Derbyshire	28. Nottinghamshire
29. Rutland	30. Yorkshire (in two parts)
31. Lincolnshire (in two parts)	32. Essex
33. Norfolk (in two parts)	34. Suffolk (in two parts)

Boldon Book (see above) has been published as No.35 in this series.

Each of the above volumes has its own indices, but J. McN. Dodgson, gen. ed., *Index to Domesday Book,* (Phillimore, Chichester, 1992), provides indices to the entire text. Its three volumes cover;-

36. Index of Places
37. Index of Persons
38. Index of Subjects

Published Domesday Book in Latin

A. Farley, ed., *Domesday Book seu Liber censualis Wilhelmi Primi regis Angliae,* (i-ii, 1783). [Often listed under 'Record Commissioners'.]
Record Commissioners, *Domesday Book seu Liber censualis Wilhelmi Primi regis Angliae,* (i-ii, ed. A. Farley, 1783, iii-iv, ed. H. Ellis, 1811, 1816).

Works discussing or using Domesday Book

The Anglo-Saxon Chronicle, (ed. D. Whitelock et al., 1961).
A. Ballard, *The Domesday Inquest,* (1906).
Domesday Rebound, (P.R.O. Handbook no.2, 1954).
H.C. Darby, *Domesday England,* (Cambridge, 1977).
H.C. Darby et al., *The Domesday Geography of England,* (5 vols., Cambridge, 1954-67).
H.C. Darby and G.R. Versey, *Domesday Gazetteer,* (Cambridge, 1975).
F.G. Davenport, *The Economic Development of a Norfolk Manor, 1086-1565,* [Forncett], (Cambridge, 1906).
R.W. Finn, *An Introduction to Domesday Book,* (1963).
H. Forde, *Domesday Preserved,* (1986).
V.H. Galbraith, *Domesday Book, its Place in Administrative History,* (Oxford, 1974).

V.H. Galbraith, *The Making of Domesday Book,* (Oxford, 1961).

E.M. Hallam, *Domesday Book Through Nine Centuries,* (1986).

J.C. Holt, ed., *Domesday Studies. Papers read at the Novocentenary Conference of the Royal Historical Society and the Institute of British Geographers, Winchester, 1986,* (Woodbridge, 1987).

F.W. Maitland, *Domesday Book and Beyond. Three Essays in the Early History of England,* (Cambridge, 1897; new edn., 1987).

C. Phythian-Adams, ed., *The Norman Conquest of Leicestershire and Rutland: A Regional Introduction to Domesday Book,* (1986).

A.L. Poole, *From Domesday Book to Magna Carta 1087-1216,* (2nd edn., Oxford, 1955).

P. Sawyer, ed., *Domesday Book: a Reassessment,* (1985).

Chapter 3

Inquisitiones Post Mortem

Introduction: Inquisitions in Latin

This is the only chapter title in this booklet which is not in English, and I hope that it will not put any readers off. It describes records which can give very valuable information about wide sections of the medieval population — about noble and gentry families, the tenants who lived on their estates and, indeed, about their local communities.

The detailed information about tenants and local communities would appear in a kind of survey, usually called an 'extent', which would be included with the *Inquisition Post Mortem*: this kind of document is dealt with in the next chapter.

The name *Inquisitiones Post Mortem* is given both to the enquiries made of panels of local jurors, and to the documents in which their answers were written down, records which were concerned with inheritance, with the handing on of landed property down the generations within the families of lords of manors. It is a curious fact that although enormous numbers of these records were made in England, they have never had an accepted English name. The nearest we have got to producing one is sometimes to turn the first word into 'inquisition', a word which has unpleasant connotations. An 'inquisition' of this kind was carried out by royal officers who were often members of the county gentry, doing this as part of their administrative work, and not by Tomas de Torquemada. (Which is not to say that being examined by them was much fun.)

But there is no great problem: the Latin name can be translated simply as 'Inquiries after death', which is just what they are: inquiries made on behalf of the government after the death of some lord. Yet for the sake of tradition I will continue to give them their established, untranslated name. And because it is a little unwieldy, I will retain the option to follow the common practice of abbreviating it to 'I.P.M.'.

The Purpose of the Record

I.P.M.s are more immediately concerned with family relationships than any other kind of medieval record, with the possible exception of wills. Feudalism made the events of family life of great importance to a superior lord. The children born to a family might one day succeed their elders as his vassals, or become the vassals of his children. They might serve as his counsellors, help to guard his castles, fight alongside him in battle, and do their level best to marry into his family.

When a vassal died, his heir should succeed in his place and take over his role and his obligations to the superior lord. The feudal structure of society made an overlord very much concerned with the family affairs of his vassals, and he had the established right to arrange the custodies ('wardships') and marriages of under-age heirs and even of widows. These were seen as reasonable rights because the superior lord needed some control over the people who were holding their manors of him and who owed him military and other services.

These were valuable rights for the overlord to exercise himself, or to give away or sell to those he favoured. The Middle Ages had no strict rule that twenty one years should be the age of majority, but anyone who could take over the running of the estates of a ten-year-old boy could look forward to several profitable years before he came to manhood. In addition, you might improve your own family's wealth and connections by arranging his marriage to a suitable girl relative, or make even more money by arranging for him to marry the daughter of another man who would pay you to have such an alliance.

(Noble women may well have gained a greater degree of personal choice after the year 1216, when King John promised, by a clause in Magna Carta, that he would not compel widows who were his vassals to remarry.)

Tenants-in-Chief

Inquisitiones Post Mortem were inquiries made after the deaths of lords, on behalf of their superior lord. But the bad news is that they were only made for *one* superior lord, the king himself, so they were not made after the death of every lord of a manor. Under the system of feudal land-holding, a lord might hold his estates from a greater lord or from the king himself. These inquiries relate only to the manors of lords who held their manors directly from the king.

This kind of record was *not* therefore made after the deaths of the great majority of lords, those who held their manors of some superior lord who, in turn, held his land of the king.

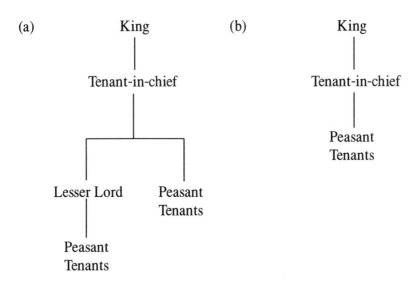

I hope that the diagrams above will help to explain this point. If the lord who has died is the lesser lord in (a), that is, a person who holds his manor or manors from some superior lord who, in turn, holds his land of the king, then no I.P.M. will be made after his death. He was not a tenant-in-chief because he had a superior lord standing between him and the king. That superior lord was the tenant-in-chief. The consequence is that we will not get details of that lesser lord's family, nor of the peasants on his manors, from this kind of source.

But if the lord who has died is the superior lord shown in (a), or the lord shown in (b), then the I.P.M. will be made, because both were tenants-in-chief. Note that a lord does not have to have lesser lords holding manors of him in order to qualify for this status: his relationship to the king is the thing which counts. Nor does he have to be a very great lord. We often think of the tenants-in-chief as very wealthy nobles with estates in several counties, and many of them were such, but there were also plenty who were ordinary members of the gentry holding just one or two manors. The consequence of their tenant-in-chief status is that we *will* get details of their families, and also (when manorial surveys survive) details of the peasant tenants who hold land on their manors.

The Making of the Records

They were made by sending royal officials to the estate of the dead lord, or to a suitable local centre where enquiries could be held. If he had been a great noble with many manors scattered across the country, then the enquiries would have had to be held at several centres, producing several accounts of his family circumstances. The officials swore in a jury of local people. These jurors were then questioned about when and where the lord had died (actual dates of deaths are sometimes given), who his true heir was, and how old the heir was.

The same jury may then have been asked to provide the detailed evidence about the manor and its people which would be made into a manorial survey.

Kinds of People Appearing

The I.P.M. will probably name the jurors but give no indication as to who they are, not even calling them 'good men and true', or some such phrase. When they can be traced in local records (such as *Manorial Court Records,* see Chapter Five) they can be shown to be prominent members of the local community — burgesses from the nearby market town, wealthy free peasants or a combination of these. Often they were tenants of the dead lord. They are the sort of people who would be serving as jurors on a manor or borough court jury where they would be called upon to exercise a fund of knowledge about local affairs.

But on this occasion their function was to answer a number of questions put to them by the officials concerning the dead lord's property and family circumstances. They were not, alas, asked to give much of the information which a modern census schedule would require. The crown's interest lay in the transmission of the estate from one generation to the next, and in the protection and exploitation of the king's rights as the feudal superior of the dead man's successor if that person were a woman or a child. The jurors were thus called upon to name the rightful heir and to give his or her age. The property was expected to descend to the eldest son, so there may have been any number of younger sons and of daughters who would not be mentioned.

But, by an odd quirk of medieval inheritance, we are given more information about the family when there are *no* sons. The story of medieval inheritance practices is much more complicated (and more interesting) than is usually

Hugh Pointz.

Inquisition taken before the King's escheator at Tockinton, in co. Gloucester, 25 January, 1 Edw. II [1308], of the lands and tenements of the which *Hugh Pointz* was seised in his demesne as of fee in the said county on the day that he died, by the oath of *John de Brockenneberg, John de Aweleye, Richard Pesson, Richard de Weston, Richard atte Home, Reginald de Juste, John le Parmenter, Robert Bosse, Adam le Chapman, Thomas atte Pull, John Smetmersch,* and *Walter le Parker,* who say that

The said *Hugh* held the manor of Tokinton in his demesne as of fee of the Earl of Gloucester by the service of 1 knight's fee.

There is there a certain capital messuage with a garden and 1 dovecote, which is worth per annum 6s. 8d. There are there in the demesne 160 acres of arable land, which are worth per annum 40s., price of the acre 3d.; also 24 acres of meadow, which are worth per annum 36s., price of each acre 18d.; also 6 acres of several pasture, which are worth per annum 6s., price of the acre 12d. There is there a certain foreign wood of oaks where there is no underwood, and it is common to all tenants of the said manor and their neighbours, and is worth nothing per annum; also a certain park with wild beasts, containing 10 acres, the herbage whereof is worth per annum, beyond the sustenation of the beasts, 5s. There is no underwood except for the enclosing of the park of the same. There are there 2 mills, which are worth per annum 20s. Sum of the demesnes per annum, 113s. 8d.

There are there 15 free tenants, who hold divers tenements in the same manor of the said *Hugh,* and pay of rent of assize 106s. 7d. at the feasts of St. Andrew, the Nativity of St. John the Baptist, and St. Michael, by equal portions. Sum, 106s. 7d.

There are in the said manor 16 tenants, each of whom holds ½ a virgate of land in villeinage. And each of them shall do between the feast of St. Michael and the Nativity of St. John the Baptist 70 manual works, and they are worth 2s. 11d., price of the work ½d., and shall do 17 ploughings during the same time, and they are worth 2s. 1½d., price of the ploughing 1½d.; and shall do from the feast of the Nativity of St. John the Baptist up to the gule of August 20 manual works, which are worth 20d., price of the work 1d.; and from the gule of August up to the feast of St. Michael he shall do 32 works, which are worth 4s., price of the work 1½d. Sum of the value of the works and services aforesaid by the year, £8 11s. 4d.

There are 12 tenants there, each of whom holds the 4th part of 1 virgate of land. And each of them shall do from the feast of St. Michael up to the feast of St. John the Baptist 70 works, which are worth 2s. 11d., price of the work ½d.; and thence up to the gule of August 10 works, which are worth 10d., price of the work 1d., and from the gule of August up to the feast of St.Michael 18 works, which are worth 2s.3d., price of the work 1½d. Sum of the value of the works and services of the same per annum. 72s.

There are there 28 cottars, who hold 28 cottages, and pay of rent of assize per annum 58s. 1d. at the 3 terms abovesaid. Sum, 58s. 1d.

The pleas and perquisites of the court, with 2 views, are worth per annum 20s.

Sum of the value of the whole extent by the year, £27 1s. 8d.

Nicholas Pointz, son of the said *Hugh,* is his next heir, and is aged 28 years and more.

Chan. Inq. p.m. 1 Edw. II. No. 46.

Figure 2. An *Inquisition Post Mortem* made after the death of a country gentleman. Most of the document is taken up by a manorial survey of the kind called an 'extent'.

supposed. It is broadly true to say that the Anglo-Saxon ruling class had practised 'multigeniture', leaving their property to a number of heirs, and that the Norman Conquest had brought a general change to a particular form of 'unigeniture' in which the eldest son emerged as the principal heir.

We should always bear in mind that property, in the form of smaller pieces of land, or cash, or goods, was also provided for younger sons and for daughters. Many ruling-class families kept to one side pieces of landed property which were not part of the family stock, but which had been acquired fairly recently and would serve as the 'portions' for younger sons or for daughters. The Kingdom of England itself served this purpose when William the Conqueror died, leaving his family land (the Duchy of Normandy) to his eldest son Robert, his acquired piece of land (England) to his second son William, and £5,000 in cash to his youngest son Henry. And, of course, much attention would be given towards securing good marriages for all the children, or places in the secular clergy or in religious houses for those who were not to marry. But the truth remains that eldest sons could usually look forward to doing much better than their younger brothers and sisters.

But relics of 'multigeniture' remained. They surface now and then down the centuries, and it would be wrong to think of Medieval England as a place where some exact set of inheritance rules was in force, or written up in some great law book just waiting to be consulted. There remained, for example, quite a frequent practice of dividing property among daughters in equal shares when there were no sons. It was for this reason that when lords died leaving no sons, I.P.M. jurors were required to provide the names and ages of all their daughters. This information was used by Professor J.C. Russell (1948) and by T.H. Hollingsworth (1969) in an ingenious attempt to reconstruct details of changes in the size of the medieval population on the basis of how many surviving children lords had in different periods.

Geographical Coverage and Dates

I.P.M.s are feudal documents made for collections of manors held by particular lords, and only for lords who held their estates directly from the king. This makes the question of their geographical coverage complicated. They survive for every English county, but in each county you will find that many places have numbers of surviving I.P.M.s, whilst the manors 'next door' have no coverage whatsoever, simply because the right kind of feudal connection did not exist between their lords and the king.

I.P.M.s were first made in the late 1230s, and they continued to be produced until the reign of Charles II, when the abolition of feudal landholding in 1660 ended their *raison d'etre.*

Survival

I.P.M.s were government records containing information of considerable interest to the crown. They were carefully preserved at Westminster, and the many thousands which survive have been published by H.M.S.O. in abbreviated form.

Pitfalls

I.P.M.s may at first sight appear as if they were made to help family historians trace noble and gentle families, but a close reading will show that this is usually only the case within narrow parameters. It cannot be stressed too much that the jurors were asked to provide very specific family evidence: the heir ('son and heir' if possible) was the person who mattered, so evidence on younger sons and on daughters is deficient. The document provides the kernel of evidence which the crown needed as feudal overlord, no more.

Readers will be pleased to find detailed evidence of medieval people's ages, but they should not be overwhelmed by this. It is a valuable indication for a society where there were no parish registers (parts of continental Europe already had parish registers, but no Englishman had thought of keeping one), but not so accurate as it looks at first sight. Professor Russell showed that many of the ages given can only be approximations: there are far too many people aged 50 or 55 and too few aged 51, 52, 53, and so on. This probably reflects the old practice of rounding off ages rather than ignorance or lack of care, but it should be borne in mind that the jurors knew more about purely local matters than about the family affairs of lords who were often absentees. Jurors who admitted that they weren't sure if such and such a daughter was the lord's true heir and that they didn't know how old she was should be commended for their frankness. If you have several I.P.M.s made in different localities after the death of one great lord (which is not unusual), then it is well worth comparing the evidence given by the different local juries.

SHORT BIBLIOGRAPHY

The *Calendars of I.P.M.s* published by H.M.S.O. (1904 onwards) give the
family details from each such document which survives in the Public Record
Office, with summaries of the landed property involved, and the names of the
royal officials and local jurors involved in making it. (They do not provide
details of manorial surveys.)

Published *Inquisitiones Post Mortem* in English translation

W.P. Baildon and J.W. Clay, eds., *Inquisitions Post Mortem Relating to
Yorkshire of the Reigns of Henry IV and Henry V,* Yorks. Arch. Soc. Rec.
Ser., lix (1918).

W. Brown, ed., *Yorkshire Inquisitions of the Reigns of Henry III and Edward
I, Vol.I,* Yorks. Arch. Soc. Rec. Ser., xii (1892).

W. Brown, ed., *Yorkshire Inquisitions, Vol.II,* Yorks. Arch. Soc. Rec. Ser.,
xxiii (1898).

W. Brown, ed., *Yorkshire Inquisitions, Vol.IV,* Yorks. Arch. Soc. Rec.
Ser., xxxvii (1906).

W. Farrer, ed., *Lancashire Inquests, Extents, and Feudal Aids.
A.D.1205-A.D.1307,* Lancashire and Cheshire Rec. Soc., xlviii (1903).

W. Farrer, ed., *Lancashire Inquests, Extents, and Feudal Aids. Part II.
A.D.1310-A.D.1333,* Lancashire and Cheshire Rec. Soc., liv (1907).

W. Farrer, ed., *Lancashire Inquests, Extents, and Feudal Aids. Part III.
A.D.1313-A.D.1355,* Lancashire and Cheshire Rec. Soc., lxx (1915).

E.A. Fry, ed., *Abstracts of Inquisitiones post mortem for Gloucestershire.
Part V. 30 Edw.I to 32 Edw.III. 1302-1358,* Index Library, (1910).

E.A. Fry, ed., *Abstracts of Wiltshire Inquisitiones Post Mortem ... in
the Reigns of Henry III, Edward I and Edward III,* (1908).

G.S. Fry, ed., *Abstracts of Inquisitiones Post Mortem relating to the City
of London, returned into the Court of Chancery. Part I. I Henry VII
to 3 Elizabeth, 1485-1561,* (1896).

H.M.S.O., *Calendars of Inquisitions Post Mortem and Other Analogous
Documents,* (many vols., 1904 onwards).

S.J. Madge, ed., *Abstracts of Inquisitiones post mortem for Gloucestershire.
Part IV. 20 Hen.III to 29 Edw.I. 1236-1300,* Index Library, (1903).

E. Stokes, ed., *Abstracts of Inquisitiones post mortem for Gloucestershire. Part VI. 33 Edw.III to 14 Hen.IV. 1359-1413,* Index Library, (1914).

Published *Inquisitiones Post Mortem* in Latin

W. Langton, ed., *Abstracts of Inquisitions post Mortem ... extracted from Manuscripts at Towneley,* [Lancashire], Chetham Soc., xcv (1875)

Works Discussing or Using *Inquisitiones Post Mortem*

T.H. Hollingsworth, *Historical Demography,* (Cambridge, 1969).

J.C. Russell, *British Medieval Population,* (Albuquerque, N. Mex., 1948).

Chapter 4

Manorial Surveys, with a Note on the Virgate

Introduction: Four Kinds of Survey

Descriptions of manors were first encountered in the Chapter on Domesday Book. Those were brief sketches giving the numbers of anonymous tenants, but the surveys made in later centuries can contain much more detail including tenants' names and, sometimes, the names of their predecessors.

These later surveys can be divided into a number of different kinds called 'custumals', 'extents', 'terriers' and 'rentals'. Each kind had different priorities and took a different form, but it is best not to read too much into a name. All were concerned to record the obligations of the tenants of a manor, and the practical differences between a custumal, an extent, a terrier and a rental might be slight according to how just much information the clerk compiling each of them chose to include. Nor have historians always drawn clear distinctions between the four.

The Purpose of the Record

Surveys were drawn up in order to show what obligations the tenants owed to the lord of the manor. Their seigneurial purpose is clear from reading them: the manor and the people who live on it are seen entirely from the lord's point of view, so that information is given on the amounts of land they hold of him and on the terms on which they hold it. How much money rent do they pay? How much unpaid work must they do for the lord? Must they give him presents, such as eggs at Easter and poultry? (Many medieval lords expected presents from their peasants.) Is the lord obliged to give them a good dinner when they work his land at harvest time?

These were important basic facts of rural life in each locality, recorded so that there was a clear record of what the lord had a right to expect, and of what each tenant had a duty to provide. They were a part of good estate management practice, and their forms and contents varied with the passage of time as estate management practices changed.

Custumals are the oldest of these records, dating back to the days of the Anglo-Saxons. A custumal of a manor will list the tenants by name, and set out the obligations which each one owes to the local lord. Thus we will find that Roger Uphill must do fifty days' unpaid work for the lord in winter, pay 1s rent at each of the 'four annual terms', and so on.

The extent is a thirteenth-century development from the days when great lords were becoming more closely involved in the working of their estates. (The oldest surviving extent made for the government dates from about 1236, and the oldest surviving private one from about ten years later.) Extents usually follow a set order, beginning with a description of the lord's 'demesne', the part of his estate which he kept in his own hands - his house, garden, dovecote, warren, deer park, barns, mills, and then his agricultural land, arable, meadow and pasture, and his woods. Then comes a description of the rest of the manor in the form of lists of the lord's tenants (most or all of whom are the local peasantry) and of the lands they hold. Unfortunately, the tenants' names are not always given. The essential feature of the extent is that it sets a monetary value on everything: the rent and unpaid labour (and anything else) which each tenant owes to the lord is given a value in cash, as, indeed, are all the assets of the lord's own demesne.

Terriers differ from the other kinds of survey in that they list the individual pieces of land which made up tenants' holdings in topographical order, going through each of the fields of the manor in turn. Individual tenants appear many times in this kind of document as each part of their holdings is listed. Some terriers overcome one of the basic limitations of manorial records: in areas where the territory of two or more estates is intermingled, they will describe the pieces of land in each field and name their tenants *whichever manor they belong to.*

Rentals are a later development, from the days when many lords of manors simply let out their property and drew rents from their tenants in modern fashion. Rentals provide lists of the tenants' names, with the sums of money which each must pay the lord, often divided according to how much is due at each of the four annual terms. Whereas custumals, extents and terriers make us think of the countryside, rentals were also a useful means of recording urban tenants and their obligations.

The Making of the Records

Manorial surveys were mentioned in the chapter on *Inquisitiones Post Mortem,* because they were often included with I.P.M.s in order to provide the government with information on the estates which a dead lord had held. But living lords of manors themselves wanted to have accurate information on their lands and rights, and so they had surveys drawn up during their lifetimes. When the widowed Countess of Lincoln resolved to manage her own estates, her counsellor Bishop Grosseteste advised her to have surveys made. The recovery of estates which the crown had seized during times of political troubles might also be a good time to commission these records.

The information in a survey, like that in an I.P.M., was often provided by a jury of prominent locals, which usually means well-off peasants. Professor Harvey (1983) found no trace of 'professional surveyors' at work in England before the sixteenth century, but there are occasional references to officials being specially brought in to make surveys. The man who surveyed a large Gloucestershire manor in the 1330s devoted 31 days to his task, and was paid 1s per day: not a princely sum, even at medieval wage and price levels, but several times what a country labourer would receive.

Manorial surveys of this date do not, alas, include any kind of map or plan. In later centuries the compiler of such a survey would have provided an excellent map as an integral part of it, but this kind of local map was extremely rare in the Middle Ages: Professor Harvey mentions a couple which survive from the fifteenth century, but notes that those were not made as parts of finished surveys.

Kinds of People Appearing

The I.P.M. was strongly concerned with the family relationships of the few, but the survey was concerned with the obligations of the many. Any information about tenants' relationships will only appear by chance — such as a reference to a tenant called 'John the son of William Broun'. But it is the record of many named tenants which provides the chief interest of this kind of document from

Redditus inter Randolsgate et Proudfoteslane et inter comunem viam Foulemergate et costram de Holbeche.

Ricardus filius Thome pro dimidia bouata sua vj*d.*
Idem Ricardus pro molelond subtus mesuagium suum ix*d.*
Rogerus Laxman pro xij. acris que fuerunt Ingeram Mosse xij*d.*
Idem Rogerus pro j. acra que fuit Simonis Alblaster iiij*d. ob. qu.*
Thomas Laxman pro iiij. acris que fuerunt eiusdem Symonis iiij*s.* in vita sua.
Heredes Thome Nel pro ij. acris que de Grymeslond ij*s.*
Idem heredes et Rogerus filius Iocei pro iiij. acris de Leneslond iiij*s.*
Petrus de Pistrina pro ij. acris viij. perticatis terre ij*s.* ij*d.* obolum ad wardam.
Galfridus filius Hugonis et parcenarii sui pro xij. acris de quarterio patris sui xij*s.*
Iohannes filius Radulfi pro iij. acris dimidia j. roda de bouata de Randolues ij*d. ob. qu.*
Willelmus de Gedney pro ij. acris j. roda de eadem j*d. ob. qu.*
Willelmus filius Ro [*sic*] Gedney pro ij. acris j. roda de eadem j*d. ob. qu.*
Thomas Laxman pro ij. acris j. roda de eadem j*d. ob. qu.*
Ricardus at Grene ⎱ pro ij. acris j. roda ad Redwelpyt ij*s.* iij*d.*
Iohannes Cotte ⎰
Filii Roberti at Stowe pro ix. acris dimidia de quarterio suo vij*s.* xj*d.*
Heredes Thome Nel pro ij. acris dimidia de eadem ij*s* j*d.*
Euerardus de Holbeche pro toto quarterio suo xvj*s.*
Ricardus Crispe pro iij. acre [*sic*] in Middeltoft ix*d.*
Ricardus filius Gerardi pro iij. acris ibidem ix*d.*
Galfridus Cryspe pro dimidia acra ibidem j*d.* ob.
Ricardus Crispe pro iij. acris ibidem ix*d.*
Iohannes Grond pro j. acra ibidem iij*d.*
Her' Ricardi Grond pro j. acra ibidem iij*d.*
Simo Grond pro ij. acris ibidem vj*d.*
Idem Simon et heredes Ricardi Grond pro j. roda ibidem *ob. qu.*
Radulfus de Flete pro xxiiij. acris de Neleslond iij*s.*
Idem Radulfus pro draua ibidem vj*d.*
Iohannes filius prebyteri pro j. acra que fuit Alani Fynche de Kaswikhirne xl*d.*

Figure 3. A Manorial Survey of the kind called a 'terrier' which listed tenants' holdings parcel by parcel, just as they lay in the fields.

the family historian's point of view. Gone are the anonymous countryfolk of 1086, the 'six cottars' and 'five bordars', replaced by John the son of William Broun and Thomas Smith the elder.

And the information provided on each person gives a basic idea of his status and place within the community. From the amount of land he holds we can tell if he is a substantial peasant with plenty of land, or a poor one struggling to survive on a few acres. The survey may reveal that he is a villein or serf burdened with the obligation to spend much of his time working the lord's own land (for no pay), or a free man with few such responsibilities and, perhaps, a very low rent. Comparison with the holdings and obligations of the other local tenants will give some insight into a particular tenant's place within local society. The poor peasant may have been a member of a whole community made up largely of such people; other communities were dominated by the local rich, or had many serfs with substantial holdings among their members. If a tenant was one of the jurors who provided the evidence from which the survey was drawn up, then he was probably an important and influential person in local terms.

Medieval surveys of manors often divide peasant tenants into their legal categories, as indicated above. It was usual to list the free men first, then the villeins or serfs. (The latter often appear under the heading 'customary tenants'.) Readers who have heard that medieval lawyers carefully divided people into those who were free and those who were not, will be surprised to find that surveys often include a *third* category, the 'cottagers' who were so poor that it didn't matter to the lord whether they were free or serfs.

The chief drawback of the record is that, however good its quality, we will only hear of the tenants, of Thomas Smith or John: their wives and children were not tenants and so were not listed (unless any grown-up children had become tenants themselves). For the purposes of the survey, they might as well never have existed. This does not mean that no women will appear. It was common for 10-20 per cent of the tenants of a manor to be women by the fourteenth and fifteenth centuries, and where it is possible to follow these women up in other local records it will be found that all (or very nearly all) of them were widows. Thus the minority of women who had become tenants themselves appear, the majority who were wives do not.

A Note on the Virgate

The sizes of tenants' holdings will often be given in terms of archaic units, of which the 'virgate' is the most common. This is a fine example of a word made up by medieval historians: the Latin original is *virgata,* and the perfectly good English word 'yardland' was available as a translation. But over the centuries 'yardland' had gradually slipped out of the language; some of the founders of the study of medieval history tried to revive it, but without success, and we are now stuck with 'virgate'.

The virgate was a piece of land big enough to make a substantial family holding. (Historians have argued about whether a peasant family would have been able to make a living from the produce of half a virgate or not.) Its size varied enormously from place to place; virgates of two or three dozen acres were common, but in some districts, such as the Cotswolds, they were often much bigger, and in others, such as East Anglia, often much smaller. Nor need the virgates of next-door manors be the same. If your source does not reveal its size, you can still make safe comparisons between the well-off tenants of a whole virgate and the much less well-off tenants of a half virgate, and assume that all of these will be much better off than the cottagers listed as holding a few acres each.

Older works on medieval history will sometimes tell you dogmatically that the size of a virgate is 30 acres. This is a relic of the Anglo-Saxon fiscal system, under which land was assessed in a notional way according to its tax liability. The post-Conquest surveys were very practical documents concerned with *real* areas of land; problems are only likely to arise when they give no indication as to how large the local virgate was or whether the local acre was a statute acre or something larger. But these problems are more likely to concern the local historian than the family historian.

Geographical Coverage and Dates

This is the first of the different kinds of manorial record dealt with in this booklet, and it is essential to repeat the word of explanation — and of caution — offered in Chapter Two. A manor was a piece of territory belonging to its lord. It might comprise a single block of land, or be made up of many small parts. It might cover the whole area of a parish, or only part of it; a very large manor might include a number of parishes. All of the village may lie within the manor, or parts of it may lie in different manors. If the family you are seeking had their land in the same parish or village but within a second manor, then they will not appear in the surveys of the first lord's estate. But you may be lucky and find a terrier which covers both.

The earliest surveys were made before the Norman Conquest, and they continued to be made throughout the Middle Ages and down into the modern period − indeed, for as long as the manor remained a real unit. As mentioned above, the various different kinds of survey were in vogue at different periods, as lords' interests in estate management waxed and waned, as local conditions and tenants' obligations changed, and as different kinds of information were collected and recorded.

Survival

It is worth making the general point that the survival of manorial records of all kinds (and from all periods) has been extremely patchy. There are excellent collections for some manors, but nothing at all for the ones next door.

Manorial surveys were valuable records, expensive to produce and full of important information about land, rights and obligations. As such, they were carefully preserved and some were periodically brought up to date, but like other manorial documents (see *Manorial Court Records*) they were subject to loss when estates moved between families or at times of political upheaval. Because of this, it is true to say that (with the exception of surveys attached to I.P.M.s and preserved by the government) it is the surveys of church estates, the manors which belonged to the great undying corporations, which are much more likely to have survived.

Pitfalls

Of all the different kinds of medieval records discussed in this little book, it is the Manorial Surveys which will bring us closest to the basic economic facts of life with which our ancestors − whether lords or peasants − had to deal. This is why it is particularly important to be aware of their pitfalls, of which there are two main ones: they may have become 'fossilized' and record conditions which actually existed generations before the date when they were made, or they may present an over-simplified picture of local landholding and society.

Drawing up a detailed and accurate survey must have taken a good deal of skill and patient work. There may have been a considerable temptation to avoid most of this by simply copying out the information given in an earlier one of the same manor, especially if the information was demanded by government agents who (being outsiders) might not notice that what they were getting was out of date. If a series of surveys reveal The Land Where Time Stood Still, then this is almost certainly what has happened. The original document will be useful (though it may not be easy to say what date it refers to) but the rest will hold little interest.

This is not the same as the practice of keeping old surveys up to date by writing in the names of new tenants and changes in their obligations. This may provide invaluable information on the successors to a particular family holding.

Not all surveys give tenants' names.

A survey which reveals that a hundred tenants have holdings of only three or four different sizes must also be viewed with caution. Such a formalized picture may have been built up from the record of tenants' obligations to the lord of the manor in his account rolls, or a similar source. The buying and selling of plots of land by the tenants, the 'peasant land market', may have made the true situation vastly more complicated. These deals may be recorded in *Manorial Court Records* or in the *Private Charters,* which we will look at next, but perhaps not in any written record.

The picture may also be over-simplified because some tenants might also hold land on the manor next door. This is particularly likely in areas where the parish or vill was divided between the estates of a number of different lords. Terriers may solve this problem, but most surveys will not.

Always read the beginning of a survey with the greatest care to ensure that it covers the whole manor: in special circumstances only a part of it may have been surveyed. One American scholar's account of conditions on a large English estate was marred by his failure to notice that for technical reasons the makers of the extent had only surveyed *half* of it. This fact was stated at the start of the document as clearly as anyone could wish.

With rare exceptions − one of which is described in McIntosh's fascinating paper (1980) − a survey was only concerned with the people who held land directly from the lord of the manor. Any of those people may have held pieces of land from eachother, i.e. as 'subtenants', which will not show up in this record. The absence of these parcels of land − which may only be tiny − is of more concern to the local historian than to the family historian, but more important is the possibility that some people may have held all their land in this way. These 'exclusive subtenants' would have held no land directly from the lord of the manor and would have had no obligations towards him, so there is no reason why they should ever have appeared in a survey. From the survey-maker's point of view they did not exist. They remain invisible, though other sources (e.g. *Manorial Court Records* or *Lay Subsidy Rolls*) may reveal their presence. A survey offers a useful list of tenants, with general guidelines to the amounts of land they held and the terms on which they held it. But its list of local tenants may not be complete.

SHORT BIBLIOGRAPHY

Harvey (1984) gives an invaluable account of the origins and development of the different kinds of survey, and of other manorial records. Lomas (1978-81) is an interesting technical survey of the development of one particular kind.

The great majority of surveys deal with manors, but urban examples have been published by Burgess (1976) and by Lancaster (1919).

Published Surveys in English (original)
J. Stansfeld, 'Rent-Roll of Kirkstall Abbey', [Yorkshire], Thoresby Soc.,
    ii, *Miscellanea Vol.I,* (Leeds, 1891), pp.1-21.

Published Surveys in English translation
W.T. Lancaster, 'A Fifteenth Century Rental of Leeds', Thoresby Soc.,
    xxiv, *Miscellanea,* (Leeds, 1919), pp.6-22.
W.T. Lancaster, 'A Fifteenth Century Rental of Rothwell', [Yorkshire],
    Thoresby Soc., xxiv, *Miscellanea,* (Leeds, 1919), pp.281-303.
W.T. Lancaster, 'Fifteenth Century Rentals of Barwick and Scholes',
    [Yorkshire], Thoresby Soc., xxviii, *Miscellanea,* (Leeds, 1928), pp.234-54.
T. Talbot, ed., *The Manorial Roll of the Isle of Man, 1511-1515,* (Oxford, 1924).

Published Surveys in Latin and English translation
L.A. Burgess, ed., *The Southampton Terrier of 1454,* (1976).

T.P. Ellis, ed., *The First Extent of Bromfield and Yale, A.D. 1315,* [Denbighshire], (1924).

J.W. Willis-Bund, ed., *An Extent of All the Lands and Rents of the Lord Bishop of St David's ... 1326, usually called The Black Book of St David's,* (1902).

Published Surveys in Latin

M. Chibnall, ed., *Charters and Custumals of the Abbey of Holy Trinity, Caen,* [Dorset, Essex, Gloucestershire, Norfolk and Wiltshire manors] (1982).

M. Chibnall, ed., *Select Documents of the English Lands of the Abbey of Bec,* Camden Soc., 3rd ser., lxxiii (1951).

M.W. Farr, ed., *Accounts and Surveys of the Wiltshire Lands of Adam de Stratton,* Wilts. Arch. and Nat. Hist. Soc., Rec. Branch, xiv (Devizes, 1958).

H.E. Muhlfeld, ed., *A Survey of the Manor of Wye,* [Kent], (New York, 1933).

N. Neilson, ed., *A Terrier of Fleet, Lincolnshire,* (1920).

S.R. Scargill-Bird, *Custumals of Battle Abbey in the Reigns of Edward I and Edward II (1283-1312),* Camden Soc., new ser., xli (1887).

Works discussing or using Surveys

P.D.A. Harvey, *Manorial records,* (1984).

R.V. Lennard, 'What is a Manorial Extent?', *English Hist. Rev.,* xliv (1929), pp.256-63.

T. Lomas, 'The development of the manorial extent', *Journal of the Soc. of Archivists,* vi (1978-81), pp.260-73.

M.K. McIntosh, 'Land, Tenure and Population in the Royal Manor of Havering, Essex, 1251-1352/3', *Economic Hist. Rev.,* xxxiii (1980), pp.17-31.

Chapter 5

Manorial Court Records

Introduction: The Private Court and its Business

In the Middle Ages, much of the judicial system had been privatised. The most important courts still belonged to the king and were held by royal judges who travelled the country on circuit or sat at Westminster, but local courts were the property of the lord of the manor. Though they had an element of a popular assembly about them, these courts were the local lord's property in just the same way as he owned his horses, his manor house and those of the local peasants who were his serfs.

As owner of the court, the lord could preside over its sittings in person, or delegate this task to an official, often called a 'steward' or 'bailiff'. No one could bring pleas against him in it, and the fines which it imposed became part of his income. (The Middle Ages had a saying, *Justicia est magnum emolumentum,* or, 'Justice is a great source of revenue'. The knack of making money out of it seems to have been lost in later times, but survives amongst lawyers.) The lord's tenants were obliged to attend. In the language of the time they 'owed suit of court', which was often clearly specified as one of the terms on which they held their land.

The Purpose of the Record

The manor court is an institution which the family historian may well have met with in a later period. It was a tough old bird, and, once established, might last for six hundred years or more. Many were still sitting in the nineteenth and early twentieth centuries, though they were getting rather stiff in their joints. Changes in land law at last made them obsolete, and only a few still meet today.

Generally speaking, this is an institution which becomes more important, and whose records become more informative, the further back in time we go. The range of business which came before a medieval manor court could be almost incredibly wide. It was both a criminal court and a civil court in an age when it seems to have been difficult to carry on peasant life and agriculture for very long without committing some minor offence or becoming involved in a dispute with the lord of the manor, his officers or one of the neighbours. And it also dealt with many matters which involved no offence, such as transfers of land, in the course of which it often recorded relationships within peasant families and even provided written records of death. (The records may contain many 'fines', but this is because the word was used in a much wider sense in those days. 'Fines' were often payments made by people taking up pieces of land or doing other legitimate actions; the payments by the guilty which we call fines usually appear under the archaic name 'amercements'.)

So many people appeared in the records of the manor court that Professor Razi (1980) has suggested that the name of every adult male resident of the manor will be there. And the evidence on some of them is good enough for attempts to be made to draw up family trees for peasant families, as the same author has done.

'Court Baron' and 'Court Leet'

The sittings of these local courts should really be divided into 'courts baron', at which local affairs were dealt with, and 'courts leet', when matters arising from the laws of England were dealt with. What often happened in practice was that the manor court met under two different guises: it might sit (say) twelve or fifteen times a year as a court baron and once or twice a year as a court leet. At the two kinds of session it would deal with different kinds of business. Or rather, it would *try* to do so, for it is by no means unusual for the same sitting of a manor court to deal with both kinds of business. Sometimes we find that the local court was making efforts to keep the two separate, even to the extent of sitting twice on the same day, once as court baron and once as court leet, but it is still likely that the business of the two will be confused in its records.

For our purposes some of these things may be just technicalities, but it is useful to know why published records which are *just* of a court baron or *just* of a court leet will differ in their contents, and why the first will usually contain much more material.

No Births, a few Marriages but quite a lot of Deaths

One function of manorial court records was to note the various kinds of payments which were due to the lord of the manor by custom. Although their main function was to secure and record his rights, notes of this kind sometimes come close to producing the sort of record we would find in parish registers.

This is particularly so in the case of records of deaths. Medieval lords frequently had the right to collect a payment called 'heriot' when one of their tenants died or (which is less well known) when a tenant surrendered his land. This payment was often taken in the form of an animal, very often 'the best beast' which the tenant or his surviving family possessed, though it might be collected in the form of money. The tenant's death (or surrender of his land) was recorded as part of the process by which the heriot was claimed and collected, and by which a new tenant was found to succeed him. The record was made very largely in order to secure the lord's rights — the right to collect heriot, the right to install the new tenant. But in so doing it provided a record of the death of an 'ordinary person' long before the first English parish register (and we must remember that parish registers record only burials, and not deaths at all).

This evidence is very useful indeed. I have never seen the exact date of a death given, but the records do occasionally state in which month a person died. Everything is consistent with these deaths normally being recorded at the manor court session held after the person died, so that, in practice, it may be possible to date a death to within a few weeks.

This seems almost too good to be true, and there are drawbacks. It is usually only the deaths of tenants which are recorded, which means that relatively few women appear and few or no children. Also, the 'heriot' was one of the obligations usually owed by villeins; freemen sometimes had to pay it, but in general their deaths are much less likely to be recorded. What proportion of the local population's deaths are actually recorded is a question which has never been answered. It probably varies a great deal from one manor to another. There are, for example, far too few deaths mentioned in the Wakefield Court Rolls for that enormous manor.

Besides receiving 'heriot' after deaths and surrenders, medieval lords received a second payment, usually called 'merchet', when women serfs married, and a third called 'leyrwite' (there are various spellings) from women serfs who were guilty of sexual incontinence. Merchet payments were given in the form of sums of money. We would think that it would be possible to use them to reconstruct marriages, but the sad fact is that they only mention the name of the woman who is to marry and (sometimes) that of her father. Only in odd cases, such as when there was a later dispute about whether the payment had been made, is there a chance that we might discover the husband's name. Free women did not owe merchet, but even so the number of such payments noted in the court records is much smaller than the actual number of marriages which must have taken place.

Leyrwite payments, also owed in the form of cash, were rare. Readers who believe in the high moral standards of the Middle Ages will be pleased to hear this. But readers of Chaucer will put it down to people not getting caught. Family historians will ask whether this kind of thing should not have been left to the Archdeacons' Courts, which were certainly functioning at this period. The answer is that the manor court was not concerned so much with matters of personal morality and questions of sin, but with infringement of the lord's property rights — women serfs (and their menfolk) being part of the livestock of his manor.

Not only were these payments rare, but the court record did not elaborate on what had taken place. For this reason, historians are still unsure just what 'sexual incontinence' means in this context. Professor Razi has suggested that leyrwite payments are effective records of illegitimate births. If that is true, then they are the only records of births that we have for the mass of the medieval population, but it must be pointed out that no record of a leyrwite payment actually mentions pregnancy or birth or the name of an infant.

We are on much firmer ground when we come to the remarriages of widows. Many widows took up their dead husbands' holdings of land and worked them themselves, becoming tenants and heads of households. In those roles, their names appear in such records as *Manorial Surveys* and *Lay Subsidy Rolls* (see Chapters Four and Seven). But many widows did remarry, and some had several husbands, sometimes in rapid succession — Chaucer's Wife of Bath is not just fiction. This kind of marriage was carefully recorded in the court records because a tenancy was changing hands. Either the widow has taken up her dead husband's land and then marries a new husband, or a new husband comes along to marry her and take up the land directly, i.e. making use of her rights in the property. The date of the marriage will not be given, but we should be safe in assuming that it took place not very long after the date of the court session at which it was arranged that the new husband would enter the land.

Before we get too carried away with the Wife of Bath, it must be said that some of the reasons for medieval widows' remarriage were very prosaic (Franklin, 1986). Economic pressure sometimes helped to drive them to it, especially the burden of doing unpaid work for the lord. Family pressures may still have influenced them. And some manor court records, such as those from the Abbot of Ramsey's manors edited by Professor Ault (1928), show the lord of the manor and his officials ordering 'young widows' to get themselves new husbands, and even setting time limits by which they must do this. We simply do not know how common this practice was.

The Making of the Records

Court records were produced by a clerk who attended the court session. He may have been a local man, or an official of the lord's who accompanied the steward from manor to manor for the sittings of individual local courts. Text books often say that manor courts were held every three weeks. Many did meet every three or four weeks (though we must not expect clockwork regularity) so that anything up to *seventeen* court sessions might take place during a single year. Others sat only twice a year, usually in the spring and autumn, when leet business was dealt with.

The written records can thus be very extensive, and it is no surprise to find that the series from the Wakefield manor court has gone into many published volumes. The records take two forms — rolls and books. Each is most commonly written on parchment, but some are on paper. Most of those which survive are neat productions which were probably written up carefully after the court sessions from original notes made at the time. The latter are very unlikely to have survived.

Court rolls and court books were made in order to show just what had taken place at the sittings of the manor court, to keep a record of the payments due to the lord for later collection, and to note changes in landholding due to deaths of tenants, purchases of pieces of land, and so on, for later reference. Although made for the lord, they could also be useful to his peasants. They might pay a fee in order to have the records searched for evidence which supported a case they had brought or for proof that they had fulfilled some obligation. As the centuries passed, it became increasingly common for local people to hold their land by means of a 'copy' of the court record, a parchment 'title deed' which

Extract from the Wakefield Court Rolls, Friday after the Octave of Easter, in the ninth year of the reign of King Edward the son of King Edward [= 18 April 1316].

Twelve Jurors. Thomas de Seyvile, Robert of Wyverumpthorp, Robert the Walker of Wakefeld, John Tasch of the same, William of Dewesbury, Richard of Birstall, Richard of Salsamara, William son of Michael of Flokton, German Filcokes, John Patrikes, Henry of Chyvet and William of Castilford, who say that,

Agnes, who was the wife of Robert Clerk of Dewesbury, brewed twice contrary to the assize, to wit a gallon at 1½d. Therefore she is amerced 6d.

Adam son of Adam Sprigonel has marked four oaks in Thurstonhagh with a certain false mark (*signum*) newly made on the pattern of the mark of the lord Earl, whereof he has felled one, worth 5s, and carried it away, and three are yet standing marked with the same mark. Therefore it is ordered that the aforesaid Adam be taken.

Robert Carpenter has caused a certain meadow of his, which is called the Olderodenge, to be enclosed by a ditch and a paling, so that the neighbours, who ought to have common in the said meadow at the proper time, after the hay is mown and carried in, are not able to use their common right as they ought to do. Therefore it is ordered that these (barriers) be thrown down.

Figure 4. Cases from a Manorial Court Record. Dating by feast days and regnal years can easily be resolved with the help of C.R. Cheney's *Handbook of Dates.*

copied the terms of their tenancy word for word. This is the origin of the terms 'copyhold' and 'copyholder'.

Kinds of People Appearing

Some people are never happier than when discovering that their ancestors were hanged for sheep stealing or transported to Australia. Others like to imagine the medieval legal system as a thing filled with vindictive cruelty, with mutilation or death lying in wait for anyone who found himself in possession of another man's halfpenny. These enthusiasts will be sadly disappointed by what they find in manorial court records. The strength of these documents lies in the great numbers of ordinary people who appear in them, many of whom have committed no crimes at all, or who are guilty of only the most trifling offences. In a world where attending the manor court's sessions was itself a common duty, appearing in the records of those sessions was a normal part of everyday life. It is obvious from reading these documents that not all of the manor's inhabitants appear: small children are unlikely to be mentioned, and far more men's names appear than women's. Studies of communities for which good records survive have also shown that wealthy members of the community appear more frequently than poor ones, partly because the local rich were more likely to serve as jurors and to be involved in the local land market. Professor Razi (see Bibliography, below) believes that all the adult male inhabitants of the manor appear in good sets of court records, but by no means all of them had such wide coverage.

The records of the manor court are primarily concerned with the manor and its people. As noted earlier, that may cover a whole parish, or may just be part of a parish or consist of scattered pieces of territory. But in either case, no English manor was ever surrounded by the Berlin Wall — people who did not live on the estate came to court to take part in cases, or might be mentioned in passing in its records. Experience shows that most of these came from the surrounding area or from manors some distance away which were the property of the same lord. Thus if records have not survived from the manor in which you are interested, it is still possible that those of another estate in the same part of the county may contain something of interest.

Geographical Coverage and Dates

There are records of this kind covering estates in every English county, but it must be re-iterated that we are dealing with the manor — a piece of territory belonging to its lord. It was not the same thing as the parish, though the two sometimes covered the same area. All of the village may lie within the manor, or parts of it may lie in different manors. If the family you are seeking had their land in the same parish or village but within a different manor, then they may not appear in its court records.

Older historians were tempted to trace the origins of the manor court back into Anglo-Saxon times because of its popular assembly element. But the oldest surviving records of proceedings in one date from no earlier than about the year 1240, and it is now generally agreed that, although the Anglo-Saxons certainly had their local meetings, the manorial court which we know is unlikely to be much older than the date of those first records. Because it played so large a part in the life of the rural community and was so very useful — both to the lord of the manor and also to local people — many manor courts continued to sit into the nineteenth and even the early twentieth centuries, so their records may extend down the centuries to within a couple of generations of the present day.

Survival

The unevenness of the survival of manorial court records is not due to one county having originally had far more than another, but because the records of large manors and of manors belonging to religious houses have been much more likely to survive the ravages of time. Some smaller manors may never have had written records of this kind, while the records of lay lords, barons and gentry, have had to survive the pitfalls of deaths, changes of family owners, seizures of estates after rebellions, and other hiatuses. Ecclesiastical manors were the properties of corporations which could not die and were unlikely to have their properties seized by an angry or avaricious king — until the 1530s when Henry VIII abolished the monasteries and many other religious institutions, and also deprived the bishops of many of their estates. But by that date conditions had changed, and many of those who acquired these former church manors were very anxious to preserve the old records which came with them.

We know of lords of manors from the Tudor period who made careful arrangements for the preservation of their old court records. At least one such nobleman, Edward Stafford, Duke of Buckingham, hoped to restore the burdens of serfdom and searched his records for proofs of which of his peasants might be claimed as serfs, for the disability was handed down from father to son through the family and had never been abolished. Less reactionary lords searched them for information on old tenancies and obligations, and sometimes had books compiled of valuable extracts and interesting cases which might serve as precedents.

Pitfalls

Good sets of manorial court records can include so many good things that readers must be warned not to expect too much.

Do not assume that because they provide coverage of many local events they necessarily record all of them. The case of the records of deaths noted above stands as a good example.

If the family for whom you are looking appear, then it is likely that they lived in the manor or not very far away. Detailed references to their landholding and activities should clear this up, or you may find them listed in a survey (see Chapter Four) or a list of taxpayers (see Chapter Seven). If they do not appear, or do so very rarely, it may be because they were poor, or lived nearby on the estate of another lord.

Be warned that the quality of court records varies enormously from century to century and from place to place. Enormous numbers of local people do often appear in them, together with some from further away. But it is very difficult to say what *proportion* of the local population really appeared because the court records are usually the most detailed documents which survive. How can we know how many more people there were if no one ever wrote their names down? Professor Poos and R.M. Smith (1984) have been able to make a comparison for a manor in E. Anglia which shows that many people who were named in lists of Poll Tax payers *never* appeared in the local court records. This must make us wary; manor courts were certainly more important institutions in some parts of the country than in others and at some periods than at others. Their records can provide a mass of detailed information, but we must not assume that this is comprehensive, nor read too much into the fact that a particular family or person rarely or never appears in them.

SHORT BIBLIOGRAPHY

Maitland (1889 and 1891) provides the classic introductions to the manor court and its records, but readers should also see Harvey (1984) and Razi (1980) for the results of subsequent research. Stuart's *Manorial Records. An introduction to their transcription and translation* (1992) is really designed for people beginning to read original records, as his sub-title shows, but offers a useful guide to understanding court records in Latin.

Published Manorial Court Records in English (originals)
J.P. Earwaker, ed., *The Court Leet Records of the Manor of Manchester ... Vol.I, from the year 1552 to 1586,* (Manchester, 1884).

F.J.C. and D.M. Hearnshaw, eds., *Court Leet Records, A.D.1550-1624,* (three parts, counting as one vol.), Southampton Rec. Soc., i (1905-07).

Published Manorial Court Records in English translation
W.P. Baildon, ed., *Court Rolls of the Manor of Wakefield, Vol.I, 1274 to 1297,* Yorks. Arch. Soc. Rec. Ser., xxix (1901).

W.P. Baildon, ed., *Court Rolls of the Manor of Wakefield, Vol.II, 1297 to 1309,* Yorks. Arch. Soc. Rec. Ser., xxxvi (1906).

W. Farrer, ed., *Some Court Rolls of the Lordships, Wapentakes, and Demesne Manors of Thomas, Earl of Lancaster, in the County of Lancaster ... A.D.1323-4,* Lancashire and Cheshire Rec. Soc., xli (1901).

M. Habberjam, M. O'Regan and B. Hale, eds., *The Court Rolls of the Manor of Wakefield, from October 1350 to September 1352,* Yorks. Arch. Soc., Wakefield Court Rolls Ser., vi (1987).

J. Harland, ed., *A Volume of Court Leet Records of the Manor of Manchester in the Sixteenth Century,* Chetham Soc., lxiii (1864).

H.M. Jewell, ed., *The Court Rolls of the Manor of Wakefield, from September 1348 to September 1350,* Yorks. Arch. Soc., Wakefield Court Rolls Ser., ii (1981).

J. Lister, ed., *Court Rolls of the Manor of Wakefield, Vol.III, 1313 to 1316, and 1286,* Yorks. Arch. Soc. Rec. Ser., lvii (1917).

J. Lister, ed., *Court Rolls of the Manor of Wakefield, Vol.IV, 1315 to 1317,* Yorks. Arch. Soc. Rec. Ser., lxxviii (1930).

G.R. Price, ed., *A transcript of The Court Rolls of Yeadon, 1361-1476,* [Yorkshire], (Draughton, 1984).

H. Richardson, ed., *Court Rolls of the Manor of Acomb, Vol.I,* Yorks. Arch. Soc. Rec. Ser., cxxxi (1969).

E. Toms, ed., *Chertsey Abbey Court Rolls Abstract, Part I,* Surrey Rec. Soc., xxxviii (1937).

J.W. Walker, ed., *Court Rolls of the Manor of Wakefield, Vol.V, 1322 to 1331,* Yorks. Arch. Soc. Rec. Ser., cix (1945).

S.S. Walker, ed., *The Court Rolls of the Manor of Wakefield, from October 1331 to September 1333,* Yorks. Arch. Soc., Wakefield Court Rolls Ser., iii (1983).

Published Manorial Court Records in Latin and English translation

F.W. Maitland, ed., *Select Pleas in Manorial and Other Seignorial Courts,* Selden Soc., ii, (1889). [Contains C13 records of Bec Abbey manors and Broughton, Hunts..]

R.A. Roberts, ed., *The Court Rolls of the Lordship of Ruthin, or Dyffryn-Clwydd, of the Reign of King Edward the First,* (1893).

Published Manorial Court Records in Latin

W.O. Ault, ed., *Court Rolls of the Abbey of Ramsey and the Honor of Clare,* (New Haven, Conn., 1928).

P.D.A. Harvey, ed., *Manorial Records of Cuxham, Oxfordshire, circa 1200-1359,* (Oxfordshire Rec. Soc., i, 1976).

R.B. Pugh, ed., *Court Rolls of the Wiltshire Manors of Adam de Stratton,* (Wilts. Rec. Soc., Devizes, 1970).

A.J. Taylor, ed., *Records of the Barony and Honour of the Rape of Lewes,* Sussex Rec. Soc., xliv (1939).

—————, *Halmota Prioratus Dunelmensis. Containing Extracts from the Halmote Court or Manor Rolls of the Prior and Convent of Durham. A.D.1296-A.D.1384,* Surtees Soc., lxxxii (1886).

Works discussing or using Manorial Court Records

J.M. Bennett, *Women in the Medieval English Countryside,* (Oxford, 1987).

E. Britton, *The Community of the Vill*, [Broughton, Huntingdonshire], (Toronto, 1977).

F.G. Davenport, *The Economic Development of a Norfolk Manor, 1086-1565*, [Forncett], (Cambridge, 1906).

E.B. DeWindt, *Land and People in Holywell-cum-Needingworth*, [Huntingdonshire], (Toronto, 1972).

P. Franklin, 'Peasant Widows' 'Liberation' and Remarriage before the Black Death', *Economic Hist. Rev.*, 2nd ser., xxxix (1986), pp.186-204.

P.D.A. Harvey, *Manorial records*, (1984).

A.E. Levett, *Studies in Manorial History*, (ed. H. Cam, M. Coate and L.S. Sutherland; Oxford, 1938).

F.W. Maitland and W.P. Baildon, eds., *The Court Baron*, (1891).

L.R. Poos and R.M. Smith, 'Legal Windows Onto Historical Populations?' Recent Research on Demography and the Manor Court in Medieval England', *Law and History Rev.*, ii (1984), pp.128-52.

J.A. Raftis, *Warboys. Two hundred years in the life of an English mediaeval village*, (Toronto, 1974).

Z. Razi, *Life, Marriage and Death in a Medieval Parish. Economy, Society and Demography in Halesowen, 1270-1400*, (Cambridge, 1980).

R.M. Smith and Z. Razi, eds., *The Manor Court and Medieval English Society: studies of the evidence*, (Oxford, forthcoming).

D. Stuart, *Manorial Records. An introduction to their transcription and translation*, (Chichester, 1992).

J. West, *Village Records*, (1962), pp.30-42.

Chapter 6

Private Charters and Quitclaims

Introduction: Charters, Deeds and Quitclaims

'Charter' is rather a vague term for a document conveying property or rights from one person or group of people to another. The charter of which we have all heard is the Great One, the *Magna Carta,* by which King John confirmed the rights which all the free men in England should enjoy. Medieval towns were happy to pay substantial sums of money for charters which granted them the rights and privileges of self-government, away from the interference of the king or of other lords.

But most of the charters written in medieval England were 'private charters' or deeds, work-a-day records conveying pieces of land which had been sold or made over as gifts from one person to another. Such charters often include evidence of relationships, and the 'quitclaims', by which people who might have claimed some rights in the land granted gave up their interests, often add more. A series of charters may make it possible to map out part of the course of a single person's life, as R. Holmes (1899) did many years ago for the twelfth-century Yorkshireman, Adam Fitz Peter of Birkin. Moreover, it may be possible to reconstruct a whole family tree from such a series, and to say a good deal about the history of the family. P. Brown (1985) has done this recently for a number of East Anglian families whose members appear in the cartularies of Sibton Abbey, Suffolk.

Many individual original charters and quitclaims do survive, the greatest collection being the thousands held in the Public Record Office. (Guides to these have been published by H.M.S.O. and by the List and Index Society.) Others are scattered through local record offices and private collections. Most of those which have been printed are not the original documents but copies which were made in collections of records which are often called 'cartularies'. The word conjures up a classic picture of a monkish writer working on parchment in the *scriptorium* (or writing office) of some great abbey, and, indeed, many such collections were put together by religious houses. But noble and gentry families also collected their records together for convenience and security, and had copies of the original documents made. Those in the hands of the Church have been more likely to survive, for the reasons I have explained elsewhere, but laymen's cartularies do survive and those made for religious houses are by no means solely concerned with gifts of land to the Church.

Readers will see from the Short Bibliography at the end of this chapter that far more cartularies have been published in the original Latin than in English. Do not be put off by this. There has for many years been a civilised practice of printing the texts of these documents in Latin with brief English summaries added to explain what is going on. I have indicated which of the works listed use this practice.

The Purpose of the Record

In the *Manorial Court Records* we can often see the tenant's family holding passing down the generations, or sometimes passing between families after a marriage. In *Inquisitiones Post Mortem* we discover who will inherit the dead lord's manor, though the document does not show them coming into possession of it. Those documents are concerned with the inheritance of the family land, the lord's manor and the peasant's holding, which provided most of their incomes and formed the basis of their family's subsistence down the generations.

In those circumstances no charter (or quitclaim) was needed. These were documents which were made when written evidence of a special kind was needed, because landed property had gone outside the family, outside the system of inheritance and marriage. In these circumstances, special records were needed to show what had taken place, to describe the property which had changed hands, to record the promise that the former holder of the land and his heirs would not try to get it back, (and, indeed, that they would support the new holder and his heirs in their right), and to give the names of the witnesses who had seen the agreement concluded.

In Norman times, and later, property transactions included symbolic actions in which one person would hand earth dug from the land itself to another. (This is why the Conqueror's seizing a handful of sand after he had fallen on the

Channel shore would have seemed symbolic to his followers.) But as literacy spread it became increasingly advisable to have written proof of one's right to land, and a charter fulfilled this function.

While there was no need to make one to record the transfer of family property down the generations, family land which was changing hands outside the inheritance system (e.g. by passing to a younger son or daughter rather than to the eldest son and heir) might well change hands through a charter. The document would serve both for land which had been, in the old phrase, 'given freely' (i.e. given with nothing received in return), and for land which had simply been sold.

The Making of the Records

Charters are one of those kinds of medieval document which the local clerk would draw up for an ordinary member of the community. They were often made at some important local centre, on a day when there would be plenty of people around to act as witnesses.

Kinds of People Appearing

Unlike *Manor Court Records* and *Lay Subsidy Rolls,* charters and quitclaims only record the names of the small numbers of people involved in the business they record. These will be the grantor, the grantee and the witnesses, or those who are giving up their rights.

The witnesses were still thought essential in most cases: written records could be forged or altered, and it was as well to have your rights also backed up by the testimony of several upright members of the community in case any dispute should arise. Relatives of any of these people might be named, especially if we are in the period before hereditary surnames have fully come into use, so that a man might be referred to as 'William, the son of Alexander de Crakanthorp', or even as 'William, the son of William, the son of Alexander de Crakanthorp'. If the boundaries of the land are described in any detail, then the names of the people whose land it borders on may be given, and, again, their relatives may be named.

The social status of those who appear may vary tremendously. There is a tendency to think of private charters as records characteristic of the ruling

Grant in free alms by Robert de Domno Martino, marshal of Boulogne, to Sibton Abbey of his windmill at Tostock, Suffolk, and of William son of Wilmer of Tostock, with his holding of land and offspring (*sequela*), and the services of William son of Roger of Norton. Dated c.1212-1229.

Sciant presentes et futuri quod ego, Robertus de Domno Martino, marescallus Bolonesii, dedi et concessi et hac presenti carta mea confirmavi Deo et Beate Marie et monachis de Sybetun in liberam et perpetuam elemosinam molendinum meum ad ventum de Thotestok, cum sede ipsius molendini, quod habui et tenui de Willelmo filio Rogeri de Nortun, et Willelmum filium Wlmerei (*sic*) de Thotestok quem habui et tenui de predicto Willelmo filio Rogeri de Nortun; ita quod predicti monachi habeant et teneant, et perpetuo iure possideant predictum molendinum, cum sede ipsius molendini, et predictum Willelmum filium Wlmeri (sic) de Thotestok, cum omni tenemento quod de me tenuit et cum omni sequela sua et cum omnibus servitiis, consuetudinibus quas mihi solebant facere, reddendo annuatim Willelmo filio Rogeri de Nortun et heredibus suis de predicto molendino, et sede ipsius molendini, ad Pasca, unum denarium, et de predicto Willelmo filio Wlmeri et tenemento ipsius ad festum Sancti Johannis Baptiste, tres obolos, et ad Natale, tres obolos, pro omnibus servitiis et auxiliis, consuetudinibus et exactionibus et questis. Testibus.

Figure 5. A Private Charter conveying not only a windmill and some land, but also the family of serfs who live on the land. Many Latin charters have been printed with English summaries.

class — of the nobles and gentry who could afford to give landed property to great abbeys, or of the king himself, whose Close Rolls preserve (amongst much other material) the texts of royal charters granting land to those he favoured. The appearance of the documents sometimes reinforces this: parchment records in neat Latin script (obviously a professional piece of work), hung with fine seals pressed into red or black wax, like the fine examples reproduced in Sir Frank Stenton's beautiful edition (1930) of Northamptonshire charters.

But this is misleading. The rich man's charter may have been more likely to survive down the centuries, but the charter was a practical work-a-day document. Its text is often both standardised and short (much shorter than many deeds of later times!). Would it take more than (say) fifteen minutes for an experienced clerk to write one out? And was there anything in its making which the local clerk who wrote the manor court rolls or his neighbours' wills could not have managed?

The property transferred could be an entire manor, but usually it was something very much smaller, often only an acre or two of land. *Manor Court Records* show us that many parts of Medieval England had thriving 'peasant land markets' in which little plots of ground were bought and sold by members of the local community. The charter was just the document to record a peasant's sale or gift. It is sad that his own, original document is so unlikely to have survived, but instances are known of lords of manors keeping copies of the records of their tenants' sales and leases, and such a document from Peterborough Abbey has been edited and published by C.N.L. Brooke and Sir Michael Postan (1960).

Nor was charter-making restricted to peasants who were free, for the title of the Peterborough Abbey collection shows that serfs could grant land by charter too. It is entitled *Carte Nativorum,* which literally means 'The Charters of the Villeins'.

Who had Seals?

We often think of the charter as the archetypal sealed document. Light-fingered eighteenth-century antiquaries have, alas, got to many of the original charters which survive and have abstracted the seal impressions which they once bore for their private collections. (And where they have got to by now is anyone's guess.) But many charters do survive with their original seal impressions, and some of the published editions of their texts — like Sir Frank Stenton's mentioned above — include reproductions of these.

We often think of seals as being a kind of badge of rank in medieval society, rather like coats of arms: the king and his nobles have them, and so do great churchmen and the local gentry. But the truth is, again, much more prosaic. A seal was a useful way of marking assent to or ownership of something. There was no rule as to who was to have or not to have them. Though the impressions of peasants' seals have rarely survived, there are some in existence which show that some members of the well-off peasantry (at least) had them.

Geographical Coverage and Dates

A charter may grant a whole manor, or a collection of manors, to someone, but it is more usual for a much smaller area of land to be concerned. Many deal with only a few acres.

The oldest examples date from not long after the Norman Conquest, but the basic form and wording of these documents was often retained down the centuries with relatively little change. Thus a charter from the time of the Tudors may look considerably older than it is. In the reign of Elizabeth I, local clerks in some areas (such as the Welsh borders) were still drawing up charters which differed very little in language and form from those made four hundred years earlier.

Survival

Where did people keep their charters? As records made for every level of society, their custody and chances of survival must have varied enormously, from the muniments room of the monastery or castle downwards. Did the peasant who held part of his land by charter keep the document in a strong-box in his house, or could he lodge it in the parish chest? In either case, the odds against its survival down the centuries must be enormous. It is likely that more charters have perished over the years than any other kind of document, and the great majority of them belonged to ordinary country people and townspeople — to the mass of the medieval English people who were our ancestors and predecessors. It is this loss of so many ordinary people's documents which has led to the widespread view that medieval records concern the rich and famous.

Pitfalls

Charters have a serious pitfall like that of wills: there is usually no reason for them to contain any mention of the bulk of a family's property, the nobleman or gentleman's manors, the peasant's main family holding, the townsman's house and shop. These things would descend by inheritance in the normal course of events: there was no need to grant them to the next generation, and there would be no charter recording their *sale* unless the family's fortunes had reached a real crisis.

Plenty of dated charters and quitclaims do survive, but it is not unusual for documents of these kinds to bear no dates. Published charters will usually have been dated roughly by their editors on the basis of the characteristics of the handwriting and the dates when the people mentioned in them are known to have been alive from other sources. Sometimes luck is on our side, and a witness will not only be named but will be recorded as having held some office at the time when he acted as a witness, such as 'A.B., then Sheriff of Borsetshire'. Given decent luck, some enthusiastic historian of Borsetshire will have produced a list of officers' names and dates from which the document can then be dated. This may appear in the Victoria County History: if it does not, then ask at the county record office.

Do not be too upset if it turns out that your charter was witnessed by two men who were not alive at the same time. The clerk (who may have been a witness himself) may have made a mistake with an unfamiliar name. Or it may be a forgery. One of the happiest memories of my education is of sitting in the late Professor Ralph Davis's palaeography class and hearing him cast doubts upon the authenticity of charter after charter as we examined them. Our forebears were not always quite as scrupulously honest as we might wish. But sometimes the situation is more complicated, as when those whose genuine documents had been lost or stolen, or left for years in damp chests until they were unreadable, had 'copies' made in order to protect their rights to property which had been gained quite legitimately.

SHORT BIBLIOGRAPHY

Far more charters have been published in Latin than in English translation, but there is a long-standing custom amongst editors of giving English summaries. I have indicated, below, which books do this.

The Descriptive Catalogue of Ancient Deeds published by H.M.S.O. (1890-1915) and the List and Index Society's Calendars and Indexes (1973 onwards) are really guides to help the reader consult original charters in the Public Record Office, rather than conventional printed editions. But they provide details of the parties involved, dates and locations of properties, and their indices are invaluable.

Brooke and Postan (1960) includes a discussion of villeins' charters by Professor Postan.

Published Charters in English translation from Latin, and English (originals)

A.H. Thompson, ed., *A Calendar of Charters and Other Documents belonging to the Hospital of William Wyggeston at Leicester,* (Leicester, 1933).

Published Charters in English translation

W. Brown, C.T. Clay, M.J. Hebditch and M.J.S. Price eds., *Yorkshire Deeds,* (ten vols.), Yorks. Arch. Soc. Rec. Ser., xxxix (1909), l (1914), lxiii (1922), lxv (1924), lxix (1926), lxxvi (1930), lxxxiii (1932), cii (1940), cxi (1948) and cxx (1955). [Abstracts].

C. Harper-Bill, ed., *The Cartulary of the Augustinian Friars of Clare,* Suffolk Rec. Soc., Suffolk Charters, xi (1991).

H.M.S.O., *A Descriptive Catalogue of Ancient Deeds, etc.,* 6 vols. (1890-1915).

List and Index Society, *Exchequer, Augmentation Office, Calendar of Ancient Deeds — Series B, Parts I-IV,* vols.95, 101, 113, 124 (1973-1976). [Vol.124 is Index.]

List and Index Society, *Exchequer, Augmentation Office, Ancient Deeds, Series BB (E.328), Calendar and Index,* vol.137 (1977).

List and Index Society, *Exchequer: Treasury of the Receipt, Calendar of Ancient Deeds — Series AS & WS (E42, E43),* vol.158 (1979).

List and Index Society, *Exchequer Ancient Deeds – DD Series, 1101-1645 (E211),* vol.200 (1983).

R.P. Littledale, ed., *The Pudsay Deeds,* Yorks. Arch. Soc. Rec. Ser., lvi (1916).

V.C.M. London, ed., *The Cartulary of Bradenstoke Priory,* Wiltshire Rec. Soc., xxxv (1979).

K.H. Rogers, ed., *Lacock Abbey Charters,* Wiltshire Rec. Soc., xxxiv (1978).

J.W. Walker, ed., *Abstracts of the Chartularies of the Priory of Monkbretton,* Yorks. Arch. Soc. Rec. Ser., lxvi (1924).

J. Walton, ed., 'The Greenwell Deeds', [Northumberland], *Archaeologia Aeliana,* 4th ser., iii (1927). (Pub. as complete vol..)

Published Charters in Latin

C.N.L. Brooke and M.M. Postan, eds., *Carte Nativorum. A Peterborough Abbey Cartulary of the Fourteenth Century,* Northants. Rec. Soc., xx (1960). [English summaries.]

P. Brown, ed., *Sibton Abbey Cartularies and Charters,* (4 parts), Suffolk Rec. Soc., Suffolk Charters, vii-x (1985-88). [English summaries.]

V. Brown, ed., *Eye Priory Cartulary and Charters, Part One,* Suffolk Rec. Soc., Suffolk Charters, xii (1992). [English summaries.]

M. Chibnall, ed., *Charters and Custumals of the Abbey of Holy Trinity, Caen,* [Dorset, Essex, Gloucestershire, Norfolk and Wiltshire manors] (1982).

G.T. Clark, ed., *Cartae et Alia Munimenta quae ad Dominium de Glamorgan pertinent,* (4 vols.), (Dowlais and Cardiff, 1885-93).

A.W. Crawley-Boevey, *The Cartulary and Historical Notes of the Cistercian Abbey of Flaxley, otherwise called Dene Abbey, in the County of Gloucester,* (Exeter, 1887).

R.R. Darlington, ed., *The Cartulary of Darley Abbey,* (two vols.), [Derbyshire], (Kendal, 1945). [English summaries.]

J.S. Davies, ed., *The Tropenell Cartulary, being the Contents of an Old Wiltshire Muniment Chest,* (2 vols.), (Devizes, 1908).

D.C. Douglas, ed., *Feudal Documents from the Abbey of Bury St Edmunds,* (Oxford, 1932). [English summaries.]

W. Farrer and C.T. Clay, eds., *Early Yorkshire Charters,* (twelve vols., later ones pub. Yorks. Arch. Soc.), (1914-65). [English summaries.]

G.H. Fowler, ed., *The Cartulary of the Cistercian Abbey of Old Wardon, Bedfordshire,* (Manchester, 1931).

M. Gervers, ed., *The Cartulary of the Knights of St John of Jerusalem in England,* (Oxford, 1982). [English summaries.]

D.E. Greenway, ed., *Charters of the Honour of Mowbray, 1107-1191,* (1972).

C. Harper-Bill, ed., *Blythburgh Priory Cartulary,* (2 parts), Suffolk Rec. Soc., Suffolk Charters, ii & iii (1980-81). [English summaries.]

C. Harper-Bill and R. Mortimer, eds., *Stoke by Clare Cartulary,* (3 parts), Suffolk Rec. Soc., Suffolk Charters, iv-vi (1982-84). [English summaries.]

H.M.S.O., *Calendar of the Close Rolls,* 47 vols. (1892-1963).

H.M.S.O., *Close Rolls of the Reign of Henry III,* 14 vols. (1902-1938).

S.F. Hockey, ed., *The Cartulary of Carisbrooke Priory,* Isle of Wight Rec. Ser., ii (1981). [English summaries.]

R. Holmes, ed., *The Chartulary of St John of Pontefract ...,* Vol.I, Yorks. Arch. Soc. Rec. Ser., xxv (1899).

W.T. Lancaster and W.P. Baildon, eds., *The Coucher Book of the Cistercian Abbey of Kirkstall,* [Yorkshire], (Leeds, 1904). [English summaries.]

A.C. Lawrie, ed., *Early Scottish Charters, Prior to A.D.1153,* (Glasgow, 1905). [English summaries.]

B.A. Lees, ed., *Records of the Templars in England in the Twelfth Century, The Inquest of 1185 with Illustrative Charters and Documents,* (1935).

R. Mortimer, ed., *Leiston Abbey Cartulary and Butley Priory Charters,* Suffolk Rec. Soc., Suffolk Charters, i (1979). [English summaries.]

J. Parker, *Lancashire Deeds, Vol.I, Shuttleworth Deeds, Part I,* Chetham Soc., new ser., xci (1934). [English commentaries.]

J.S. Purvis, ed., *The Chartulary of the Augustinian Priory of St John the Evangelist of the Park of Healaugh,* Yorks. Arch. Soc. Rec. Ser., xcii (1936).

U. Rees, ed., *The Cartulary of Haughmond Abbey,* [Shropshire], (Cardiff, 1985). [English summaries.]

U. Rees, ed., *The Cartulary of Shrewsbury Abbey,* (two vols.), (Aberystwyth, 1975). [English summaries.]

C.D. Ross and M. Devine, eds., *The Cartulary of Cirencester Abbey, Gloucestershire,* (3 vols.), (Oxford, 1964-77). [English summaries.]

F. M. Stenton, ed., *Facsimiles of Early Charters from Northamptonshire Collections,* Northants. Rec. Soc., iv (1930). [English summaries and excellent facsimilies of original documents.]

R.T. Timson, ed., *The Cartulary of Blyth Priory,* [Nottinghamshire],
    (1973). [English summaries.]
G. Wrottesley, ed., *Chartulary of Dieulacres Abbey,* [Staffordshire], (1906).

Works discussing or using Charters

C.N.L. Brooke and M.M. Postan, eds., *Carte Nativorum. A Peterborough Abbey
    Cartulary of the Fourteenth Century,* Northants. Rec. Soc., xx (1960).
R. Holmes, 'The Charter-History of a Long Life. Adam Fitz Peter of Birkin',
    Thoresby Soc., ix, *Miscellanea,* (Leeds, 1899), pp.56-61.
W.G. Hoskins, *The Midland Peasant,* (1957).

Chapter 7

Lay Subsidy Rolls, with a Note on the Vill

Introduction: the Importance of the Taxes of 1290 to 1334

Though it now sounds too much like a dream of Merrie England to be true, there was once a time when the ordinary Englishman (or woman) was rarely called upon to pay any tax. The lord of the manor would demand his rent and manor court fines (and a host of other payments), the Church would demand tithes and offerings, but the government rarely asked for the contributions which have since become so popular.

It was Edward I's wars with the Scots and French which changed this situation, creating a huge need for money which the king's Jewish moneylenders and Italian bankers found it impossible to fill. Widespread taxation was the only available means of raising anything like the huge sums needed, and this began on a large scale in the year 1290. It did not become regular, but it did become frequent, and taxes were sometimes raised in consecutive years.

This new tax system required the names of every single taxpayer to be recorded. Each time the tax was raised, a small army of amateur taxmen scoured each county for taxpayers and wrote down the names of every single one on parchment rolls which are often thirty or forty feet long — the Lay Subsidy Rolls. The system, which now seems incredibly cumbersome, was kept up in this form until the year 1334, when the authorities flew to the opposite extreme and decided to stop assessing each individual taxpayer and just to assess each settlement. Local people were then left to sort out amongst themselves just who should pay what. The records produced under the new system were still called Lay Subsidy Rolls, but the old detail was gone — they had plenty of place-names but no names of taxpayers.

This is the importance of the period from 1290 to 1334, for it was between those years that taxpayers' names were recorded in huge numbers — as many as

16,000 per county per tax — in a kind of record which is available in print for many English counties. It is with the specially-informative records of this period that this chapter will deal.

The Purpose of the Record

The purposes of the Lay Subsidy Rolls were stated quite clearly in the instructions which Parliament issued to the chief tax collectors (or 'chief taxers') in each county. They were to have them drawn up in order to help them collect the tax, and they were also to send copies to Westminster so that the Exchequer could keep an eye on the process and would know how much it could expect to receive. If the examination of a Roll suggested any kind of malpractice, then the chief taxers could be ordered to come to the Exchequer and there be hauled over the coals, though in practice this seems rarely to have happened.

It is interesting to note that the Exchequer seems to have regarded these rolls very much as work-a-day documents which would be useful while each tax was being collected, but of little further interest thereafter. It was not until thirty years after this tax system had started that an official was appointed to preserve them as records, and the loss of earlier ones may suggest that they were not even being kept to compare the revenue of succeeding taxes.

The Making of the Records

The rolls which Parliament ordered the chief taxers to have made covered the whole of their counties and gave each taxpayer's name and assessment. But the sources from which they took their information were more detailed records, sometimes called 'detailed local rolls', in which their subordinates had written down not only the taxpayers' names, but also exact details of how their assessments had been worked out. Thousands of these lists must have been made, but few have survived. Most of those which are left cover only a few dozen taxpayers from one settlement, or from a single urban parish. Some of these have been published, and are indicated in the Short Bibliography below.

Compiling the two kinds of list — the 'detailed local rolls' for each area and the finished 'county rolls' for the whole shire — must have been a major task for the amateur taxmen, and it is likely that they had the use of the sheriff's office in the county town and the help of his clerks.

The Raising of the Taxes

Once the chief taxers for each county had been chosen (usually from members of the local gentry with administrative experience), they appointed small groups of local people to act as taxmen (called 'subtaxers') in the various divisions of the county. Most of these groups dealt with one hundred each, but separate groups were often appointed to deal with each major market town, while great cities like London, Bristol and York required a number of groups.

The lay subsidies of this period were not poll taxes, to be paid by every adult, nor were they taxes on incomes nor on land. Instead, they were levies on 'movables', on people's personal possessions. Just what possessions were taxable was not made clear in the instructions sent out to each county. The authorities were probably relying on the local taxmen to follow instructions which had been issued in earlier times. The 'detailed local rolls' which survive show that countryfolk were usually assessed on the value of their animals and corn. Townsmen were assessed on many more items: on their animals and corn, on the equipment for their trades, and on domestic articles such as silver spoons, bedding and cooking pots. Their rural neighbours rarely paid tax on such things.

The tax was set in terms of fractions, which varied considerably during the period. In 1290, for example, one fifteenth of the value of every taxpayer's possessions was demanded, but in 1327 one twentieth. The local taxmen went around their districts valuing their neighbours' movables, and when each man's goods were valued that sum was divided by the fraction at which the tax had been set. Thus a man with possessions valued at (say) 60s would have had to pay 4s in 1290 or 3s in 1327.

In some, but by no means all, years a system of dual fractions was in operation. Taxpayers who lived in some of the major towns and on manors which belonged (or had once belonged) to the crown were made to pay at a higher rate than everyone else. This became a regular feature of the system in 1334, when the higher rate was standardized at one-tenth and the lower rate at one-fifteenth. (This is why, from 1334 onwards, these taxes became known as the 'Tenths and Fifteenths'.) The printed rolls for each county show clearly at what rate the tax was being levied, and whether inhabitants of some towns and manors were having to pay at a higher rate.

How fair were these taxes? Comparative studies have suggested that there was a great deal of under-assessment, in the sense that taxpayers were paying much less than they should have done. Professor Harvey (1965) was able to value the goods of the lord of the manor of Cuxham, Oxfordshire, from the lord's own records and prove that he was let off very lightly. The same manorial records show the taxmen being given sums which are usually said to be bribes, though some of them may have been legitimate contributions towards their expenses. (It is important to note that the lay subsidies were assessed and collected by amateurs who received no pay for their labours.) But whether many people who should have paid tax were able to escape paying, so that their names were not recorded, is a more difficult question, and one which historians have still to resolve.

But it is worth noting that studies of that kind have focussed on the Lay Subsidy Rolls from the later part of the period, when many taxpayers were paying only a couple of shillings, and some as little as 6d. The impact of these taxes must have been much heavier in the 1290s, when they were producing much more money for the Exchequer. But we know little yet of any organised resistance to them in England, and they certainly never sparked off protests like that which greeted the last medieval Poll Tax.

It has been observed that as time passed there was a common tendency for the yield from each county to fall and for the numbers of taxpayers listed to decrease, but no one has yet been able to prove whether this was due to increasing resistance to the taxes, growing corruption amongst the taxmen or increasing poverty amongst the payers.

A Note on the 'Vill'

Enormous numbers of historical records treat England as a collection of rich men's estates or of ecclesiastical units – they are concerned with manors or with parishes. But medieval tax records view the country in a different light: they are concerned with its administrative division into counties, hundreds and *vills*. Counties are still with us today, though there were many small changes in boundaries even before the local government reorganisation of 1974. Hundreds (often called 'wapentakes' in the North of England) remained in existence until the late nineteenth century, and they often loom large in older county histories and in the Victoria County History for each shire, where details of their boundaries and histories can be found.

But readers may not have encountered the 'vill' before. It is an awkward word to translate: the medieval clerks borrowed the classical Latin word *villa* (which we often still think of as meaning a country house, though its meaning in Roman times was actually much wider). The Middle Ages used *villa*, or sometimes *villata*, as a very elastic term which could cover a city, a town, a village or a collection of the tiniest rural settlements. It would be tempting just to translate it as 'settlement', but this is very vague. 'Town' in the old sense of the word, which has left us with expressions such as 'London Town', carries the right feeling, but it is now archaic and to apply it to great cities and hamlets alike sounds eccentric. The reader may like to use the old term 'township', but medieval historians have taken an easy option and turned the clerks' *villa* into 'vill'.

An urban centre can simply be described as a vill. In country districts, the relationship between the vill and the manor is not always clear. The lists of taxpayers' names in lay subsidy rolls sometimes show clearly that large manors are being divided up into vills and that small ones are being grouped together in order to form vills.

Kinds of People Appearing

These taxes were called *lay* subsidies because they were raised from the laity. In theory, the clergy were taxed separately, though in practice it was hard to get the system to work so neatly, and a lay subsidy roll will usually include a few clergymen's names.

Very few of the tens of thousands of people listed are given personal titles or have their occupations noted, but it is clear that they are a mixture of lords and peasants in the countryside, and townsfolk in the urban centres. E. Britton (1977) has suggested that rural taxpayers were overwhelmingly lords of manors and well-off peasants, but a recent study followed up a sample of taxpayers in manorial records and showed that many poorer peasants were also paying these taxes and so having their names listed (Franklin 1993).

The lists are not really those of tenants (though in practice most of them would have held land), nor yet lists of all adults — for these are not poll taxes — but rather lists of the names of some heads of households.

Though titles are rarely used, the position of names sometimes marks social distinction. In some districts the clerks had the practice of putting the local lord of the manor at the top of a list of taxpayers. If the taxpayers of a large manor were divided between a number of lists covering different vills, then the clerks who used this practice might put the lord's name at the head of one list and those of wealthy local peasants at the heads of the others. But beware, for other clerks seem to have put people of importance at the *foot* of lists and the two practices can sometimes be found in the same rolls!

Often about 90 per cent of the names in each county roll are those of men. The remaining ten per cent of taxpayers who are women were also the heads of households, and when it has been possible to trace them in manor court records it has been shown that most or all of them were widows. Lay subsidy rolls from some parts of the country show much lower proportions of women taxpayers — about 5 per cent on parts of the Welsh and Scots borders and only 1 per cent in Lancashire. This may partly reflect lawless conditions which made it hard for women to maintain independent roles, or older patterns of social behaviour in which nearly all widows had remarried leaving very few as heads of households.

Geographical Coverage and Dates

Each roll covers a whole county, with odd exceptions noted below, but there are no rolls of this kind for Cheshire or County Durham, because they had special status and their inhabitants did not pay this kind of tax. The northernmost counties were sometimes exempted because they had suffered greatly in Scots raids. The system was extended from England to parts of Wales in the early 1290s, where it helped to produce the great Welsh uprising of 1294-95.

Remember that the 'historic' county and hundred boundaries were not fixed and immutable. Many detailed changes took place over the centuries, and you may find that the lay subsidy roll for your county includes places which were transferred to others many years ago and fails to include the locality which interests you.

Survival

We might have expected records concerned with government income to be treated like gold dust, but this was not the case with these tax rolls. Indeed, in some ways the Exchequer seems to have been slow to cope with this new, frequent taxation. It was regarded at Westminster as a special source of revenue,

BRISTOL

(*VILLA BRISTOLL*)

Redcliffe Quarter (*Quarterium de la Radeclyve*)

6

Name	Tax		Name	Tax		Name	Tax
William Hayl	12s		Roger Pebbelewe	8s		John le Preyour	8s
Roger Stapelton	3s		Nicholas de Pridie	4s		William Warman	6s
Robert Westb'	8s		Richard Plomer	3s		John de Dene	2s
Robert Stapelton	5s		Richard de Stoke	4s		Hugh le Proute	10s
William Thornbury	5s		Robert Fenel	2s			
Robert Geryng	12d		John Welysshote	4s		Total, 42s	
Thomas atte Hulle	8s		Richard Heyne	4s			
John Kerdyf	3s		Walter Malleden	12d		Approved. Total of the twentieth of	
Adam Welyshote	4s		Margaret Rondulph	4s		the said Redcliffe Quarter with the	
Everard Fraunceys	20s		John atte Merssh	3s		subtaxers' taxes, £26 16s 8d	
John North	8s		Hugh le Tylar	12d			
William de London	3s		Richard Leyr	8s			
John de Keynesham	43s		Richeman de Welles	40s		**All Saints' Quarter (*Quarterium***	
Roger Teslare	16s		John Hugges	4s		***Omniorum Sanctorum dicte Ville***	
William Edward	2s		John Methelan	7s		***Bristoll*)**	
Agnes Curteys	8s		Robert Muleward	4s			
William Bruges	2s		Philip Standissh	8s		8	
John Wermenstr	2s		William Wasshema	2s		Henry le Taillur	2s
Christine Mauduyt	4s		Simon Webbe	4s		Robert Cocus	12d
John Wycombe	6s		Walter de Welles	14s		Richard Bryan	18d
			Henry de Welles	3s		John de Stoke	18d
			Thomas Hendy	5s		Thomas le Sullar	5s
			Robert le Heyward	2s		Roger le Gurdlar	12d
			Richard Bel	6s			

Figure 6. A Lay Subsidy Roll listing individual taxpayers by local areas.

aside from normal government income, and it was not until 1323 that an official was appointed to look after the 'county rolls'. This is probably the reason why many more survive from the 1327 and 1332 taxes than from those of earlier years.

It appears that only the county rolls which were sent to Westminster survived, eventually coming into the safe-keeping of the Public Record Office. The few detailed local rolls which are left are usually ones which had been delivered to Westminster — an unusual event which may suggest that the authorities were suspicious of their contents.

Pitfalls

So many names appear in tax rolls that it would be easy to treat them as complete lists of heads of households. Comparison with local records from the same areas shows that this is not the case. Different studies have suggested that between c.40 and 63 per cent of rural household heads paid these taxes. The wealthier local inhabitants were most likely to appear, but some of the poorer peasants also had to pay.

Nor should too much be read into the amounts which people were required to pay. By the later days of the system these were often far smaller than what a realistic appraisal of their possessions would have produced. This may be put down partly to bribery and partly to the complicated workings of under-assessment. The most detailed records suggest that the amateur taxmen used low valuations, conventional valuation (by which I mean counting every sheep as worth 1s, every quarter of wheat as worth 4s, and so on, instead of valuing every individual sheep and quarter of wheat, as they should really have done), and the ignoring of some possessions to produce low tax assessments for their neighbours.

To modern eyes this looks either inefficient or scandalous, but the officials of the medieval Exchequer allowed the system to continue for many years. It is very hard to believe that they did not know what was going in. The truth may be that they were willing to countenance it because the system did produce substantial sums of money relatively quickly, and without the risk of a widespread popular uprising.

SHORT BIBLIOGRAPHY

Willard (1934) is the standard book on the Lay Subsidy Rolls of 1290-1334, but is mainly a work of administrative history. What proportions of household heads or families paid tax, and just who the taxpayers were, are discussed in Britton (1977) and Franklin (1993). The reality of tax assessments is dealt with in the introduction to Harvey (1959) and in Harvey (1965). Some of the rare 'detailed local rolls' have been printed in Brown (1894), Fuller (1894-5), Powell (1910), and Raftis and Hogan (1976).

The standardised tax assessments which were introduced for all the vills in England in 1334, but which give no taxpayers' names, are printed in Glasscock (1975).

Published Lay Subsidy Rolls in English translation

D.A. Crowley, ed., *The Wiltshire Tax List of 1332,* Wilts. Rec. Soc., xlv (Trowbridge, 1989).

P. Franklin, *The Taxpayers of Medieval Gloucestershire,* (Stroud, 1993).

R.E. Glasscock, ed., *The Lay Subsidy of 1334,* (1975).

Published Lay Subsidy Rolls in Latin

J. Amphlett, ed., *Lay Subsidy Roll, A.D.1332-3, and Nonarum Inquisitiones, 1340, for the County of Worcester,* Worcs. Hist. Soc. (1899).

W. Brown, ed., *Yorkshire Lay Subsidy: Being a Fifteenth Collected 30 Edward I (1301),* Yorks. Arch. Soc. Rec. Ser., xxi (Leeds, 1897).

W. Brown, ed., *Yorkshire Lay Subsidy: Being a Ninth Collected in 25 Edward I (1297),* Yorks. Arch. Soc. Rec. Ser., xvi (1894). [Detailed Local Rolls].

A.C. Chibnall, *Early Taxation Returns,* Bucks. Rec. Soc., 14 (1966).

M. Curtis, 'The London Lay Subsidy of 1332', in G. Unwin, ed., *Finance and Trade under Edward III,* (Manchester, 1918), pp.35-92.

E. Ekwall, ed., *Two Early London Subsidy Rolls,* [1292 and 1319], (Lund, Sweden, 1951).

F.J. Eld, ed., *Lay Subsidy Roll for the County of Worcester, I Edward III (1327),* Worcs. Hist. Soc. (1895).

C.M. Fraser, ed., *The Northumberland Lay Subsidy Roll of 1296,* Soc. of Antiq. of Newcastle upon Tyne (1968).

E.A. Fuller, 'The Tallage of 6 Edward II. (Dec. 16, 1312) and the Bristol Rebellion', *Trans. Bristol & Glouc. Arch. Soc.,* xix (1894-5), pp.171-278. [Detailed Local Rolls].

A.T. Gaydon, *The Taxation of 1297,* Beds. Hist. Rec. Soc., xxxix (Streatley, 1959).

S.H.A. Hervey, ed., *Suffolk in 1327: Being a Subsidy Return,* Suffolk Green Books, ix (Woodbridge, 1906).

S.H.A. Hervey, ed., *Two Bedfordshire Subsidy Lists, 1309 and 1332,* Suffolk Green Books [sic], xviii (Bury St Edmunds, 1925).

W. Hudson, ed., *The Three Earliest Subsidies for the County of Sussex in the Years 1296, 1327, 1332,* Sussex Rec. Soc., x (1910).

A.D. Mills, ed., *The Dorset Lay Subsidy Roll of 1332,* Dorset Rec. Soc., Pubn. No.4 (Dorchester, 1971).

J.W.R. Parker, 'Lay Subsidy Rolls, 1 Edward III. Yorkshire North Riding and City of York', Yorks. Arch. Soc. Rec. Ser., lxxiv (1929), *Miscellanea Vol.II,* pp.104-71.

E. Powell, *A Suffolk Hundred in the Year 1283,* (Cambridge, 1910). [Detailed Local Rolls].

J.A. Raftis and M.P. Hogan, *Early Huntingdonshire Lay Subsidy Rolls,* (Toronto, 1976). [Detailed Local Rolls].

A.R. Rumble, ed., *The Dorset Lay Subsidy Roll of 1327,* Dorset Rec. Soc., Pubn. No.6 (Dorchester, 1980).

J.P. Rylands, *The Exchequer Lay Subsidy Roll ... in the County of Lancaster, A.D.1332,* (1896).

K. Williams-Jones, *The Merioneth Lay Subsidy Roll 1292-3,* Board of Celtic Studs., History and Law Ser. No.29 (1976).

J.W. Willis Bund and J. Amphlett, eds., *Lay Subsidy Roll for the County of Worcester, Circ. 1280,* Worcs. Hist. Soc. (1893).

Works discussing or using Lay Subsidy Rolls

M.W. Beresford, *The Lay Subsidies and Poll Taxes,* (Canterbury, 1963).

E. Britton, *The Community of the Vill,* (Toronto, 1977), pp.70-6.

P. Franklin, *The Taxpayers of Medieval Gloucestershire,* (Stroud, 1993).

J.F. Hadwin, 'The Medieval Lay Subsidies and Economic History', *Economic Hist. Rev.,* 2nd ser. xxxvi (1983), pp.200-17.

P.D.A. Harvey, *A Medieval Oxfordshire Village, Cuxham 1240 to 1400,* (Oxford, 1965).

J.R. Maddicott, *The English Peasantry and the Demands of the Crown, 1294-1341,* Past and Present Supplement No.1, (Oxford, 1975).

S.K. Mitchell, *Taxation in Medieval England,* (ed. S. Painter; New Haven, Conn., 1951).

M.C. Prestwich, 'Edward I's Monetary Policies and their Consequences', *Economic Hist. Rev.,* 2nd ser., xxii (1969), pp.406-16.

M. Prestwich, *War, Politics and Finance under Edward I,* (1972).

J.F. Willard, *Parliamentary Taxes on Personal Property, 1290-1334. A Study in Mediaeval English Financial Administration,* (Cambridge, Mass., 1934).

J.F. Willard, 'The Scotch Raids and the Fourteenth-Century Taxation of Northern England', *Univ. of Colorado Studs.,* v (1908), pp.237-42.

J.F. Willard, 'Side-lights upon the Assessment and Collection of the Mediaeval Subsidies', *Trans. Royal Hist. Soc.,* 3rd ser., vii (1913), pp.167-89.

Chapter 8

Wills

Introduction: The Success of the Medieval Will

The various kinds of record discussed in this little book grew out of specifically medieval conditions. They had their origins in medieval society and were part of that society's practice of record-keeping. No one in the modern world would send out clerks to compile a new *Domesday Book* or would make new *Lay Subsidy Rolls.* It is true that *Inquisitiones Post Mortem, Manorial Surveys* and *Court Records,* and *Private Charters and Quitclaims* continued to be drawn up long into the modern period, but that marked the success of medieval institutions which proved very tenacious of life. Yet such institutions gradually declined and their records became stereotyped or verbose, losing much of their original importance and interest as the centuries passed.

Wills form the exception to this pattern. Far from declining as the centuries have passed, they have continued to be made in great quantities and in very much the same form, so that at first it is hard to think of them as medieval documents. Yet this is really a case of a kind of medieval record which has retained a tremendous popularity. Although the Anglo-Saxons made a kind of will, the English will with which family historians are familiar took on its essential features in the hundred years before the reign of Edward I. Many of its essential features have changed little since that time, so that reading a medieval will can seem to put us in touch with a remote period to a remarkable extent.

This is also because of the personal nature of the will. Medieval people speak to us all the time, but it is often the voice of officialdom speaking in the third person. Wills are not the only records to speak in the first person – charters tell those who see or hear them what lands 'I, Roger Carpenter' have granted to someone – but a testator's last wishes have a uniquely personal content, which is reinforced by the fact that many of these documents were actually written in the English of the day.

It is true that their contents are affected by the conventions of the time, but it is partly the ways in which these conventions differ from those of later wills which help to distinguish the medieval will from its modern descendant.

The Purpose of the Record

The maker of a medieval will aimed to dispose of the things which were his (or hers) to give away as he (or she) pleased. To modern eyes, these things make up a very curious list, beginning with the soul, continuing with the body and only then moving on to more worldly things like land, money and household possessions. At first, no distinction was made between a 'testament' which dealt with money and other 'movables', and a 'last will' which dealt with land, but from the fourteenth century onwards some testators did produce two separate documents which followed this division.

The obvious thing which we might expect to appear, the family's main holding of land, may not be mentioned at all. It would descend to the widow or heir by widow's right or by inheritance. That process did not need a will and was not to be interfered with by one, though by the fifteenth century there was a growing tendency to include the main piece of family land within the will. When a will follows the older practice, the eldest son may cut a very poor figure, receiving little or nothing not because of some terrible family quarrel but because his birthright will come to him automatically.

Testators did not have complete freedom in making their bequests. The custom of leaving one-third of the dying man's property to his widow, one-third to his children and one-third just as he pleased (which readers may have met in a later period) was quite widely followed, especially in the North of England (see G.G. Alexander, 1928).

Will-making was strongly encouraged by the Church for a host of both spiritual and practical reasons. The first provision of a will was that in which the testator left his soul to God Almighty, the Virgin Mary and all the saints; the second was that in which he provided for the Christian burial of his body in a particular church or churchyard. Alms-giving had been encouraged by the Church for centuries as a form of penitence for sins. Gifts given during the sinner's lifetime were especially encouraged, but it was clear that many people preferred to hold onto their property and only relinquish it when death was near.

This was a major reason for the development of the will, and a major reason why it was the church courts which came to superintend them. The bequests in a will took part of the dead man's property outside his family, and the family might not be too pleased to lose some of their inheritance. It was useful to have a written statement of his last wishes and the authority of the Church to back it up.

Church courts were anxious to protect alms-giving (the Church itself was often a beneficiary) and in the twelfth and thirteenth centuries they established regular procedures for dealing with disputes, controlling executors and ensuring the delivery of bequests. It became accepted that wills were Church business, and the royal courts do not seem to have objected to this.

The Making of the Records

For many years there was a strong tradition of will-making on the death-bed, a tradition which survived into the early modern period. Cases are known of medieval people who made a number of wills on different occasions, but this was unusual except for those (such as pilgrims and mariners) who were going on long or hazardous journeys. The making of a will was usually seen as an important part of the process of dying, of the 'Art of Dying' as it became in the last plague-ridden part of the Middle Ages.

The parish priest (or a more exalted cleric for a member of the ruling class) would usually have been there to help the testator prepare for death, and he was the natural person to help with the making of the will. He probably encouraged pious bequests, and sometimes acted as a witness and as an executor. It was usually him or the parish ckerk who wrote out the will, though some ruling-class wills were the work of notaries.

After the testator had disposed of his soul and his body, and made his bequests, he then appointed one or more executors, and sometimes a number of overseers to advise them and superintend their work. A wealthy person might appoint a series of executors to act for him in the different parts of the country where his property lay, and name a group of 'counsellors' who were to advise them.

The names of the witnesses were then recorded. Only two or three witnesses were actually needed, but most testators wanted more, and lists of ten or more names are not uncommon in fourteenth-century wills. When the will was complete, the executors often sealed it with their seals.

Probate

When the testator had died, it was the responsibility of the executors to take his will along to the church court and pay a fee for its services. The witnesses might also be required to go along so that they could be examined and the will could then be 'proved'.

As with so much in this field, it was the thirteenth century which saw the development of an efficient system of getting wills implemented. The probate procedure before the church court established the validity of the will and its exact contents. Then an inventory of the deceased's possessions was drawn up, and the executors were given authority to pay out the bequests.

Many ecclesiastical authorities established their rights to grant probate: bishops, their officers, cathedral chapters, archdeacons, rural deans, and even some rectors of individual parishes. It soon became apparent that getting probate could be slow and costly when someone died leaving property in a number of different jurisdictions, and this is the origin of the system of prerogative courts. In such cases it became established that when the property lay within a single diocese, probate was reserved to the bishop or his official. When it lay in several dioceses, it passed to the jurisdiction of the archbishop. The result was an efficient system by which probate was granted quickly and records of the terms of the original wills were kept at central registries. It is usually these copies which have survived when the original documents have long perished.

This efficiency often enables us to date deaths to within a few weeks. Actual dates of deaths are unlikely to be given, but wills are usually dated and the date of probate usually follows not long after. The death must have occurred sometime between the two dates.

The texts of wills can sometimes be found in other places, some of which may seem surprising. Professor Levett (1938) showed that on the Abbey of St Albans' estates free men's wills were proved before the local archdeacon, but those of serfs were proved before the abbey's cellarer *sitting in the manor court* and their texts were then written up in the court roll.

Charitable Bequests

Charitable provisions were a feature of many medieval wills. Gifts to the Church were usually mentioned before bequests to family members, and were certainly one of the basic reasons why the Church had become involved in the regulation of wills. The dying man would leave money or goods to the repair of his local parish church, to particular altars in the church, and perhaps also to the cathedral of the diocese. He might also make bequests to particular religious houses: the different orders of friars were very popular by the Later Middle Ages. The sums involved are often modest, but it is the remembering which counts.

Wealthy testators, however, might spend considerable sums on their funerals and on provision for masses and prayers to be said for the benefit of their souls for many years after their deaths. Those who had vowed to go on a crusade or a pilgrimage but had never fulfilled the obligation could make arrangements in their wills for substitutes to make the journeys on their behalf.

Money is often left also for distribution among the poor, if the testator can afford it. There may be a penny for each poor person who attends the funeral. There is also sometimes support for other causes which now seem less charitable, such as the making and repair of roads and bridges. Medieval will-makers made provision for welfare payments and other works which the medieval state could not finance.

Kinds of People Appearing

Will-making was so strongly encouraged by the Church that, in theory, every adult should have done it. (And for this purpose adulthood was taken to begin at age 14 for men and at age 12 for women, the minimum ages at which marriage was possible.) Yet we may wonder what proportion of adults met with sudden deaths which gave them no chance to make wills and how many of the dying were still clear enough in mind and memory ('of a good and perfyght remembraunce') either to dictate their detailed provisions or to give proper assent to them. I do not think that these questions have ever been properly addressed. Some church court registers do contain long lists of intestate deaths, recorded so that executors could be appointed.

The Will of William Davy, Fishmonger and Citizen of London, 1426

In the name of god, amen. In the xxvij day of november, The yere of our lord M CCCCmo xxvj, I, William Davy, Fyschmongere and Citezyn of London, In hool mynde, make and ordeyne my Testament in this maner,

Ferst, I bequethe my sowle to almyghty god and to al the seyntis, my body to be beryed in the Chercheyerd of seynt Clementis be syde Est chepe,

Also, I bequethe to the werkes of the forseyd cherche, xl s,

Also, I bequethe to the persone of the sayde cherche, xiij s iiij d,

Also, I bequethe to the mayster clerke, iij s iiij d,

Also, I bequethe sere Wilyam Podon, iij s iiij d,

Also, I bequethe sere Iohn Buk, iij s iiij d,

Also, I wele that every prest that is at my dyrige and at messe have vj d,

Also, I bequethe Margrete Schiplake, xl s,

Also, I bequeth Waket, prentys with Schiplake, vj s viij d,

Also, I bequethe Iohn Davy, my brother, xl s,

Also, I bequethe Margery, my sister, xx s,

And the residue of al my godys, after my testament is fulfyllyd and my dettys payd, they be disposyd for my soule after the disposicion of my executour, and to this I make and ordeyne William Schiplake, Barbour, myn executour, and I bequethe the same William, xl s,

Also, yeve hym withowte that, for hese laboure, vj s viij d,

Item, I bequethe Iohn Lowesley, vj s viij d,

Wittenessis, sere Andrewe Norwiche, persone, and Thomas Rokewode, clerk.

Figure 7. A Will with typical medieval features, yet much that is familiar from later centuries.

Medieval lawyers (who came to take up some odd standpoints when struggling to make logical sense of the consequences of the growth of serfdom) declared that serfs could not make wills because all their property belonged to their lords. Medieval history has had a strong legal bias since its beginnings as a serious study, so the reader may well come across this view in older text books. Yet a study of local records shows that it is incorrect: serfs could and did make wills. In fact, on some estates they were required to make them because the lord of the manor would seize all their possessions if they died intestate!

Wives have been seen as a group with very limited freedom to make wills because most of their property was considered to be their husbands'. Medieval lawyers usually argued that they had little scope to bequeath property and should always have their husbands' permission, but the wills which survive often show a more liberal position with married women leaving personal effects and property which had belonged to their own families. The strong opposition to Christians dying without making wills may have encouraged this trend.

Medieval will-makers certainly came from a wide range of social backgrounds, from the royal family (some of whose wills were printed by J. Nichols as long ago as 1780) down to humble peasants and craftsmen. The question which no one has yet answered is what *proportion* of the 'humble peasants and craftsmen' made them. Professor Gottfried (1978) argued from the enormous numbers of fifteenth-century East Anglian wills which survive that it was a very high proportion. His view would certainly have pleased the church authorities, but proof is difficult.

A medieval will is partly a family document, with the charitable bequests which the testator can afford added on. The people named in it are usually the testator himself, those who receive bequests, the executors and the witnesses. The cleric who actually wrote the document may be named separately, if he was not among the executors or witnesses. Those receiving bequests will usually be close relatives of the dying man, though properous people often also left money or goods to faithful servants. Clergymen's wills are often interesting because they make up for the lack of children of their own by remembering those of their siblings with bequests to 'John, the son of my brother Walter' and so on.

The executors are also often close relatives. It was common practice to appoint several of them, sometimes with elaborate arrangements for who was to take over if any of them died 'in office'. Husbands and wives usually appointed their surviving partners; children and clergymen were also popular choices.

Witnesses could be found among the testator's friends and neighbours. Local custom sometimes required particular officials to be witnesses, such as the mayor in a borough (if land was being bequeathed) or the lord of the manor's bailiff for a serf's will.

In addition, the names may be given of the people to whom the dying man owes money, and also of the man who actually wrote the document. Other local people may be mentioned in passing: the people from whom he bought pieces of land which he is now leaving may be mentioned in order to help identify the properties.

Dates

The Anglo-Saxons made wills of a kind, and an interesting collection of these has been published by Dorothy Whitelock (1930). But the will of the later medieval and modern periods grew up in the late twelfth and early thirteenth centuries. Professor Sheehan (1963) has traced its development in a fascinating technical study.

Survival

Wills were made by individual people and handed over to their executors. The odds must be heavily against the original documents having survived down the centuries. Bundles of them have sometimes come into the possession of record offices, but they usually survive only in the copies made for the church authorities.

The involvement of the Church, with its well-trained administrators and good record-keeping practices, has resulted in the survival of large numbers of late medieval wills from some parts of the country. Professor Gottfried's study (1978) of disease mortality in East Anglia was based upon about twelve thousand fifteenth-century wills which have survived in the church archives.

A.J. Camp (1974) lists the dates from which the earliest wills in particular bishops' and archbishops' registers survive, and these are often in the fourteenth century or the latter half of the thirteenth. But not all of these documents have been put into print.

Pitfalls

A will may provide an invaluable part of a family tree, but it will probably not be a very extensive one. Medieval Englishmen left their possessions to their widows and children, and sometimes to surviving siblings, nephews and nieces. With a few exceptions (such as godchildren and servants) people outside a narrow family circle rarely received bequests.

It is dangerous to read too much about a family's wealth and social position into a will, because its main piece of property – the lord's manor, townsman's shop or peasant's family holding – would descend automatically to the next holder and would often not be mentioned at all.

Do not assume in this (or any later) period that because people did not appear in a will they did not exist, nor infer too much about personal relationships from the fact that Agnes was left only 12d and Thomas was not mentioned at all. The heir may cut a poor figure because the will does not concern itself with his inheritance. Children may receive very little from their father's chattels because their widowed mother's death will bring them much more in the course of time. Or they may be left little at the end because they have already been well provided for, they have received their 'porcions'.

Keep medieval piety in perspective. Alms-giving now looks picturesque, and it may certainly reflect a genuine desire to do some good in the world. But in times when it was the common practice, a testator's last good deeds may not tell us much about his particular beliefs or personality. We might bear in mind that the Church was aware from an early date of those who lived evil lives and sought to make recompense only at the very end, with a definite hint of bribing divine justice!

SHORT BIBLIOGRAPHY

Medieval wills were one of the first kinds of document to interest local record societies, and great numbers have been printed in both English and Latin. The lists below can offer only a selection.

Readers who begin to find thirteenth- and fourteenth-century wills too modern for their taste should look at D. Whitelock (1930), where some *really* old ones are printed in Old English with a parallel translation. M.M. Sheehan's book

(1963) is a technical study of the development of the English will, but contains some fascinating information.

Published Wills in English

F.J. Furnivall, ed., *The Fifty Earliest English Wills in the Court of Probate,* *London,* E.E.T.S., Original Ser. 78 (1882, reprinted 1964).

G.J. Piccope, ed., *Wills and Inventories from the Ecclesiastical Court,* *Chester,* (3 vols.) Chetham Soc., xxxiii, li, liv (1857, 1860, 1861).

——, *Testamenta Eboracensia. A Selection of Wills from the Registry at York,* *Vol. VI,* Surtees Soc., cvi (1902).

——, *Wills and Inventories from the Registry at Durham, Part II,* Surtees Soc., xxxviii (1860).

——, *Wills and Inventories from the Registry at Durham, Part III,* Surtees Soc., cxii (1906).

Published Wills in English, and in English Translation from Latin

I. Darlington, ed., *London Consistory Court Wills, 1492-1547,* London Rec. Soc., iii (1967).

C.W. Foster, ed., *Lincoln Wills Registered in the District Probate Registry at* *Lincoln, A.D.1271 to A.D.1532,* (3 vols.) Lincoln Rec. Soc., v, x, xxiv (1914, 1918, 1930).

E. Roberts and K. Parker, eds., *Southampton Probate Inventories 1447-1575,* (2 vols.) Southampton Rec. Ser., xxxiv and xxxv (both 1992). [Contains Glossary.]

F.W. Weaver, ed., *Somerset Medieval Wills (1383-1558),* (3 vols.) Somerset Rec. Soc., xvi, xix, xxi (1901, 1903, 1905).

Published Wills in Latin and English (original)

R.B. Cook, ed., 'Wills of Leeds and District', Thoresby Soc., xxiv, *Miscellanea,* (Leeds, 1919), pp.304-35. [Some Anglo-French.]

R.B. Cook, 'Wills of the parishes of Rothwell, Saxton, Sherburn in Elmet, Swillington, Thorner, Whitkirk and Woodkirk', [Yorkshire], Thoresby Soc., xxxiii, *Miscellanea,* (Leeds, 1935), pp.22-60.

G.D. Lumb, ed., *Testamenta Leodiensia, 1514-1531,* (three parts), [Leeds], Thoresby Soc., ix, Miscellanea, (Leeds, 1899), pp.81-96, 161-92 and 246-77.

——, *North Country Wills, Being Astracts of Wills Relating to the Counties of York, Nottingham, Northumberland, Cumberland, and Westmorland at Somerset House and Lambeth Palace, 1383 to 1558,* Surtees Soc., cxvi (1908).

——, *Testamenta Eboracensia. A Selection of Wills from the Registry at York, Vol.III,* Surtees Soc., xlv (1865).

——, *Testamenta Eboracensia. A Selection of Wills from the Registry at York, Vol.IV,* Surtees Soc., liii (1869).

——, *Testamenta Eboracensia. A Selection of Wills from the Registry at York, Vol.V,* Surtees Soc., lxxix (1884).

——, *Wills and Administrations from the Knaresborough Court Rolls, Vol.I,* Surtees Soc., civ (1900).

——, *Wills and Inventories ... of the Northern Counties of England from the Eleventh Century Downwards, Part I,* [Durham], Surtees Soc., i (1835).

Published Wills in Latin

A.E. Levett, *Studies in Manorial History,* (ed. H. Cam, M. Coate and L.S. Sutherland; Oxford, 1938), pp.208-34. [Includes some serfs' wills in Latin].

J. Nichols, ed., *A Collection of the Wills of the Kings and Queens of England from William the Conqueror to Henry VII,* (1780).

——, *Testamenta Eboracensia or Wills Registered at York ... from the Year MCCC. Downwards, Part I,* Surtees Soc., iv (1836). [A few Anglo-French.]

Works Discussing or Using Wills

G.G. Alexander, 'The Custom of the Province of York. A Chapter in the History of Wills and Intestacies', Thoresby Soc., xxviii, *Miscellanea,* (Leeds, 1928), pp.417-30.

A.J. Camp, *Wills and Their Whereabouts,* (4th edn., 1974).

R.S. Gottfried, *Epidemic Disease in Fifteenth Century England,* (Leicester, 1978).

J.D. Hanna, *The Canon Law of Wills,* Catholic University of America Canon Law Studs., lxxxvi (Washington, 1934).

A.E. Levett, *Studies in Manorial History,* (ed. H. Cam, M. Coate and L.S. Sutherland; Oxford, 1938), pp.208-34.

F. Pollock and F.W. Maitland, *The History of English Law before the time of Edward I,* (2nd edn., 2 vols.; Cambridge, 1911).

M. Sheehan, *The Will in Medieval England. From the Conversion of the Anglo-Saxons to the End of the Thirteenth Century,* (Toronto, 1963).

Index